BOBBY COLLINS

THE WEE BARRA

BOBBY COLLINS

THE WEE BARRA

DAVID SAFFER

TEMPUS

To my wife Betty and my children Robert, Michael and Julie.

FIRST PUBLISHED 2004

Tempus Publishing Ltd
The Mill, Brimscombe Port
Stroud, Gloucestershire GL5 2QG
www.tempus-publishing.com

© David Saffer, 2004

The right of David Saffer to be identified as the Author
of this work has been asserted in accordance with the
Copyrights, Designs and Patents Act 1988.

British Library Cataloguing in Publication Data.
A catalogue record for this book is available from the British Library.

ISBN 0 7524 3176 5

Typesetting and origination by Tempus Publishing
Printed and bound in Great Britain

CONTENTS

ACKNOWLEDGEMENTS

Grateful thanks to the following people and organisations for their help with this publication: Betty, Davie and Archie Collins, Jeanette Kelso, Bertie Auld, Brian Labone, John Giles, Norman Hunter, Tommy Henderson, Leeds United Football Club, Mike Fisher at Yorkshire Post Newspapers Ltd; Gordon Lock, Vincent Gillen, Richard Share; James Howarth and Holly Bennion at Tempus Publishing Ltd.

Images for this publication have been supplied by Yorkshire Post Newspapers Ltd, D.C. Thomson & Co. Ltd, The *Scottish Daily Record*, *Scottish Daily Express*, UPPA, Stan Plus Stan Two and West Riding News Service. Every effort has been made to identify the original source of other illustrations. For questions regarding copyright contact Tempus Publishing Ltd.

Finally, both Bobby and myself would like to thank statistician Gary Shepherd for producing all the career statistics for this book. His expertise and efforts are greatly appreciated.

PREFACE

Fifty-five years ago I made my debut for Celtic in a League Cup clash against our great rivals Rangers. The journey that followed took me around the world as I made my way in the game. Winning to me was everything and I believed in playing the game hard but fair, and expected the same in return. Of course, the clubs I played for enjoyed varying degrees of success, as was the case when I became a coach and manager, but I always gave my best.

At Celtic, although we didn't dominate through the 1950s, I'm proud of the trophies we won when the likes of Charlie Tully, Willie Fernie, Jock Stein and Neil Mochan thrilled supporters. Winning the Scottish Cup in 1951 was unforgettable because it was my first major honour and our championship success in 1953/54 was particularly special because it was gained over an entire campaign. However, for a one-off performance, no Celtic player or supporter will ever forget the day we defeated Rangers 7-1 to win the League Cup in 1957. Everything we tried came off and the whole occasion is one of my favourite memories.

After moving south to Everton in 1958, we arguably underachieved with the squad we possessed, but there were many memorable performances. When the opportunity came to join Leeds United in 1962 everyone thought I was crazy joining a team destined for the Third Division, but Don Revie was adamant his young players had potential, and he was proved correct.

Reaching an FA Cup final for the first time in the club's history was a superb achievement, but just being part of the birth of Don's great side, which included players such as Billy Bremner, Jack Charlton, Norman Hunter and John Giles was sensational; you could sense the club was going places. The overall highlight though was the Footballer of the Year award I received in 1964/65 when we so nearly claimed the double. Not only was I the first Leeds United player to win the prestigious trophy, but also the first Scot.

Representing the Scottish Football Association and Scotland meant everything to me. My fifteen-year association with the international team enabled me to test my skills against world stars such as Stan Matthews, Alfredo di Stefano and Ferenc Puskas, and compete in the 1958 World Cup finals.

I'm delighted that David has pieced together my football career in this book. Although I embarked on my footballing journey more than five decades ago I wanted as many images included as possible and accurate statistics. On both counts David has done a grand job.

Finally, I would like to thank my old friend Bertie Auld for his kind words and all the contributors for their reminiscences.

Recalling my career has been wonderful; I hope you enjoy reading the final result.

Best Wishes
Bobby Collins

Bobby Collins

INTRODUCTION

During the 1950s and 1960s few players in British football made a bigger impact on the game than Bobby Collins. After making his debut for his hometown club Celtic in 1949, Bobby went on to serve the Glasgow giants with distinction for the best part of a decade, winning League Championship, Scottish Cup and League Cup honours. Throughout much of this period Bobby was a regular for the Scottish League representative XI and the Scotland's full international side, culminating in his participation at the 1958 World Cup.

Joining Everton after the finals in Sweden, following a four-year spell where he skippered the team, Bobby joined Don Revie's Leeds United team who were lying at the bottom of the Second Division. During five years at Elland Road, Bobby helped establish the club in the higher echelons of the First Division and to an FA Cup final for the first time in the club's history. Bobby is today acknowledged as Revie's greatest ever signing.

Following his departure in 1967, Bobby offered his vast experience to Bury and Morton before embarking on a number of player-coach and managerial roles in Australia and England. This overview however, barely scratches the surface of what was unquestionably an extraordinary career.

The 'Wee Barra', as he was affectionately dubbed by Celtic followers, endeared himself to both players and supporters alike with his all-action game. A brilliant tactician and motivator, Bobby was a supreme passer of the ball and possessed a thunderous strike, bamboozling many a goalkeeper with his trademark 'banana' shot. Though one of the smallest players around, Bobby made his presence known in every game and never shirked a tackle. His reputation preceded him, but there was little opponents could do. Playing with and against the great stars of a golden era, Bobby held his own against the elite.

Unfortunately I didn't see Bobby play at his peak, but in my discussions with players, supporters and observers of football, everyone speaks with the utmost respect about a footballer who was quite simply a 'winner' in every aspect of his game.

Enjoy the memories.

David Saffer

FOREWORD

Bobby Collins was a model footballer and a major influence on me during my career. He was in the Celtic team when I broke into first-team football and was a member of the Scotland XI when I won my first cap against Holland.

Bobby made me feel so welcome at Celtic from the start. I remember him giving me his Adidas boots from the 1958 World Cup finals. They were slightly big for him at the time but they were my first major manufacturer's pair. I was the envy of all the younger players breaking through in the squad!

Bobby was great with the young kids at Celtic. In the late '50s there were no full-time coaches as such, we had a manager who selected the team, although he was influenced by the chairman, and we had a physio. The coaches were the more experienced players. The club had a particular dress code and Bobby looked the part both on and off the pitch. He was always immaculately dressed and a model professional. Everyone admired him.

We got on really well both on and off the park. Bobby made you feel so important because he realised that the reserves today were the first-team players tomorrow. A number of us at the club, Billy McNeil, Steve Chalmers and myself went on to become part of the Lisbon Lions. Others such as Pat Crerand starred at Manchester United. Bobby helped us all.

On the park, if things were going wrong, he was always encouraging and a great source of inspiration. It was brilliant being in the same team as Bobby, but a nightmare for opponents! He never stopped you from expressing yourself, and if you had a bad game or made a mistake he would be the first to offer alternatives. You could not help but admire him.

Bobby was a winner. He was also a manager's dream because he could play in various positions, but in my opinion he was devastating at inside right. Bobby was physical and a wee bit robust but he was not a dirty player. His all-action game meant that he picked up injuries that would have finished most players, but Bobby always came back stronger. His strength of character was astonishing.

There were so many games when Bobby had a major impact. I remember when Celtic won 4-1 at Rangers in a cup match. Bobby controlled the game from start to finish; he was immense, and then in my first international against Holland he was again outstanding. One other game that has to be recalled was again against Rangers, this time in the 1957 League Cup final, when we won 7-1. Unfortunately for me after playing in all the earlier rounds, I missed out on that famous occasion and had to play in a reserve match against Queen of the South, but I've seen a film of the game and it was one of those days when everything went right and Bobby was at the hub of everything positive. He was incredible.

Whenever Celtic supporters recall great stars from the '50s, they nominate the Wee Barra. The term 'legend' is used far too much these days, but not in the case of Bobby Collins, both as a team player and as an individual. His name is up there with the very best, and I know it's the same at both Everton and Leeds United where he was just as sensational.

Bobby played outside right, inside right, in fact he could play across the forward line, and of course he also starred in midfield. Bobby Collins could have graced a team in any era; he was one of British football's greatest stars.

Bertie Auld

ONE

FOOTBALL CRAZY
1931-1949

Born in Glasgow on 16 February 1931, Bobby was the eldest child of Tom and Bella Collins. Alongside brothers Davie, Tommy, Archie and sister Janette the Collins family grew up at 26 Polmadie Street. A fourth brother Samuel died when he was a baby.

Football was always the path that Bobby was going to take; his formative years saw him play for Polmadie Primary School, Calder Street Secondary School, Boys Brigade football, Polmadie Hawthorns and finally Pollok Juniors.

My local team was Third Lanark and I first saw them play when I was around seven. I went to games with my brother Davie; we'd sneak in by squeezing under the fence!

Happy Days! Bella and Tom Collins' wedding day. Seated are Bobby's future relations Aunt Beeny and Uncle Samuel, 1930.

Bouncing babe, 1931.

During the war years I remember watching wartime internationals at Hampden. Little did I realise I'd play with and against some of the stars, and at the stadium itself. One match in particular I recall was when Scotland beat England 5-4. It was a pretty rare occurrence during the wartime clashes as England generally got the better of the results but this was a match to savour.

I was really influenced by players of the era and among a host of Scots we cheered on were the likes of Jimmy Delaney, Billy Liddell, Archie Macauley, Jimmy Caskie, and two players who went on to manage at the highest level, Bill Shankly and Matt Busby. England were spoiled for choice and over the years I saw Eddie Hapgood, Stan Cullis, Joe Mercer, Stan Matthews, Frank Swift, Raich Carter, Jimmy Hagan and Tommy Lawton display their skills.

I played at every opportunity and growing up I loved hearing about the likes of Hughie Gallacher, Alex James and Jimmy Mc'Mullan who proved that height did not matter if you are good enough. This trio all represented Scotland with distinction during the 1920 and 1930s.

Third Lanark's ground, Cathkin Park, was close to Hampden Park and across the road from Cathkin was where I played for the Life Boys, Boys Brigade and our local district team, Polmadie Hawthorns. Being so close to these stadiums you could not help but dream of playing there one day. I went on to represent my hometown junior team, Glasgow Pollok, who played at Newlandsfield. Although it was an ash pitch the facilities were different class to what I'd been used to. Playing for Pollok you were watched by scouts. My height was often discussed but it didn't concern me. I knew that like Gallacher, James and Mc'Mullan if my skills were up to scratch they'd be spotted.

Brothers Davie and Archie recall growing up in Polmadie.

Davie: 'It was hard for my parents during the war years; however we had a happy childhood. Bobby and I, like all the boys in the district, played football in the streets, the park, anywhere we could. We used a tennis ball, put coats down for posts and we were away.

'I remember Bobby playing for the eighth battalion of the Boys Brigade in other inter-battalion matches before he went through the ranks. Like all kids, we got into mischief, stealing apples and pears, and got into the usual scrapes that boys do. They were not easy times, but everyone helped each other out. Our only claim to fame was that film star Mickey Rooney was born across the road from us, although he had moved some time before to America to make his name. Bobby loved football and we watched local games whenever possible.

'We used to watch Third Lanark (not the greatest side but a hard side to beat) and games at Hampden Park. We also went to other major events; one occasion was a boxing flyweight title match between Peter Kane and Jackie Patterson at Cathkin Park; it was great fun.'

Chief Indian. Bobby, 1935.

That's my boys! Bobby and Davie with their dad, c. 1940.

Bobby (second left, third row) is pictured with the Boys Brigade, c. 1941.

Archie: 'Bobby was always very protective towards me as I was five years his junior, and anyone who hit me soon knew about it. His life was football and he'd always be practising in the streets for hours. Bobby's hero was Third Lanark inside forward Jimmy Mason, who was a great little player.'

Childhood friend Tommy McGrotty recalls: 'From the age of eight, Bobby and I looked after his dad and Uncle John's pouter pigeons. Football was always going to be his career though. I remember arranging for him to play for the Boys Brigade in Pollok Shaws. We won 20-0 and Bobby scored 10!'

Being successful at schoolboy and youth level made Bobby a targeted youngster, however the background to his arrival at Celtic was astonishing because he put himself out of the junior game for six weeks and landed his new manager, Jimmy McGrory, in trouble with the Scottish Football Association.

I was only seventeen and had been getting rave reviews at Pollok. A number of clubs were interested, including Everton, who invited me for a trial. I went south with my dad and things went well. Everton negotiated a £1,000 transfer fee with Pollok, a record at the time for a junior, but the night before I was due to head south, Jimmy McGrory came to my home and told me he wanted to sign me. I was thrilled. The next morning l told Everton's representative Robert McMurray and Pollok secretary Willie McGahan that I wanted to sign for Celtic.

Bobby duly signed for his hometown club but Everton officials demanded an investigation. As Bobby had signed amateur forms the Scottish Football Association refused to accept Celtic's registration documents and the Scottish League was forced to step in and adjudicate. They ruled that Bobby was an Everton player, a decision ratified by the Scottish Football Association when they viewed the correspondence

Bobby shows off his cobbling skills.

15

between Everton and Pollok. They duly rapped Celtic manager Jimmy McGrory for his actions. While Bobby waited, the Scottish Junior Football Association pointed out that however binding the correspondence appeared; the only agreement in football that was truly binding was a player's registration form, not amateur forms. As the arguments continued, eventually, Everton waived their claim. To get around the bureaucratic rules Bobby re-signed for Pollok, played against Blantyre Celtic and then signed officially for Celtic!

It took a few weeks but I was determined to stick it out because I only wanted to play for Celtic. I signed as a part-time player on £8 a week because I was still an apprentice cobbler.

TWO

WEE BARRA
1949-1953

Having arrived at Parkhead, Bobby made his bow in a trial match. Local reporters were impressed. 'It looks as if Celtic are going to find the wait worthwhile,' wrote one journalist. 'Fifteen thousand were quick to take him to their hearts and he was cheered by shouts of "Gi'e us some more, Bobby!" long before the finish. He was quick, elusive and accurate with his passing.' Another paper noted: 'There was no showmanship about Bobby's work, but there was plenty of intelligence. It looks as if Celtic have found themselves a first-class little player.'

It didn't take the newcomer long to make his debut as Bobby was selected to play outside right against Rangers in a League Cup clash on 13 August 1949. Following Celtic's 3-2 win, the youngster's performance was well received by the media.

Scott Hall: 'A wonderful little fellow, perky up-and-at-'em Bobby Collins, stepped into football yesterday. Veteran Jock Shaw, of Rangers, gave the little fellow a warm hug as the pair of them walked off at the end. This was a fine compliment, for the darling will-o'-the-wisp out on Celtic's right wing, had, with this, a baptismal performance, given old-timer Jock one of his greatest 'toastings'. Collins, who takes a size four boot, is a cobbler by trade. He certainly showed the Rangers defence cobbled heels yesterday. This was a happily moving co-operative Celtic team that played fast, fighting football. Collins was a first-appearance little hero.'

Bobby commented on the match in a number of articles.

What a way to begin my Celtic career... a clash against our greatest rivals. Before the game everyone wished me well. Bobby Evans told me to just play my natural game, which was what I needed to hear. I was determined to show everyone what I could do. When we ran out the noise was incredible. There were 70,000 in the stadium and the atmosphere was fantastic. I've played all over the world but there is nothing that compares to an Old Firm clash. I was fortunate that this would be the first of many for me and I relished them all. The game went well for us. I managed to win a penalty, which John McPhail converted before Mike Haughney grabbed the winner.

A thrilling 5-4 win over Aberdeen, a match in which Bobby grabbed his first goal for the club, was the perfect start to the competition, but three consecutive defeats ended Celtic's participation. Nevertheless, following his League debut against Queen of the

South, Bobby grabbed his first League goal, and the winner, in a 3-2 win against Hearts.

John Jessiman of the *Sunday Express* observed: 'Little Bobby Collins, game as a pebble, built like a Brencarrier, and in his element at inside right, crashed home a picture opportunist goal, fired first time. Away up on terracing behind the goals, out flew the green scarves. He brings back to Celtic, this boy, the immortal fire of Patsy Gallagher. His idea of progress is the shortest way through… the technique of the electric drill! When he was not hurling himself at the entire Hearts defence he was back defending. That was Patsy's way. After the Collins winner, the roar from the Parkhead faithful went on for five minutes. No wonder!'

A 4-2 win at home to Aberdeen saw Celtic among the early pacesetters after 6 games. Rex's Parkhead Story in the *Sunday Mail* said: 'The greatest thing that has happened to Celtic in post-war years is Bobby Collins. Just the right height for leanin' on if he'd stay still long enough! When you watch John McPhail tapping the ball out to the wee chap, taking the return and sending it back to him again, you think of Faither taking his wee jewel doon tae the sands tae sail his wee boat. The difference here is that Boy Collins often leaves Faither McPhail and has a go at launching a battleship! I can't remember this wee spark, who looks like the last cigarette in a packet of Woodbine, losing one ball that was legitimately his, and I can remember him grabbing the ball when it was legitimately someone else's. I hope he doesn't go big in the head; I don't think he will. For if ever a lad was playing for Celtic first and Collins a long way second, this was he.'

It was an impressive start to Bobby's professional career, but despite his side's promising opening, inconsistent form saw Celtic finish the season in fifth place behind Champions Rangers. Missing only 4 games, Bobby grabbed 7 goals, including a penalty against Hibernian in a 4-1 defeat. His strike was the only successful spot kick of five awarded in the game and he had to take his twice!

Nevertheless, Bobby had made his mark. Strong, determined and possessing a never-say-die attitude, fans loved his style of play and dubbed him the 'Wee Barra'. During the post-season Celtic embarked on a trip to Italy to play Lazio in a prestigious friendly to commemorate Holy Year. Travelling by ferry to France, players met legendary crooner Bing Crosby before completing their journey by train to Rome, where the squad were invited to visit the Vatican, before battling to a 0-0 draw with Lazio. In articles of the era, Bobby recalled:

My early games for Celtic went well and I soon settled into the team's pattern of play. Before I knew it I'd been switched to inside right, so now I was expected to play as a linkman in attack as well as a striker who had to get his share of goals. It was a challenge, but if the manager thought I was capable of playing in that role then that was fine by me.

There was no over-complication in tactics. Talk never centred on 4-2-4, 4-3-3, diamond formations or sweeper systems, we believed in attacking football. That was

Opposite: Teenage sensation (© D.C. Thomson & Co. Ltd)

Mr. ROBERT KELLY, J.P.

Chairman of Celtic Football Club; President
of the Scottish Football League; and Vice-
President of the Scottish Football Association.

LEAGUE CUP
Saturday, 13th August, 1949
Kick-off 3 p.m.
Celtic v Rangers

No. 1   PRICE 3d

Tough debut.

our style of play. If we were on the attack we'd have five forwards and two wing halves looking for opportunities and supporting each other. If we were on the defensive we'd track back to support our defenders.

Of course we had players who could control a game; intelligent footballers like Bobby Evans, Willie Fernie, Charlie Tully and John McPhail, and with players of this calibre in the side changing tactics came natural to us and we were able to adapt. If we had to battle we could and if we were able to play our natural game we did.

In 1950/51, Celtic's League campaign was again inconsistent and ultimately wrecked by 5 consecutive defeats after New Year. Finishing seventh, some 19 points adrift of champions Hibernian, the second half of the campaign would see just 4 wins. One area in which Bobby had proved himself was as a goalscorer. Leading the way in the League with 15 goals, Bobby scored in consecutive victories against Morton, Clyde, Falkirk and Airdrie. He also grabbed his first hat-trick in a 6-2 win against East Fife.

The clash against East Fife was a remarkable match that saw Celtic open the scoring on six seconds with a John McPhail strike. As for Collins' treble, his first goal came when he linked up with Weir and McPhail, the second was a tap in after Weir's shot had struck the crossbar, his hat-trick goal, and Celtic's sixth, was a fine strike following a square ball from McPhail, who also scored three.

If the League campaign was disappointing, results were better in domestic cup competitions. In the League Cup, Celtic reached the knockout stages for the first time

Collins challenges Partick Thistle's Gibb. Also pictured are Kennell (Partick) and Peacock (Celtic).

since the competition's inception in 1946, before going out at the quarter-final stage against Motherwell.

In the Scottish Cup, expectancy grew round by round as Celtic overcame East Fife (after a replay), Duns, Hearts, Aberdeen and Raith Rovers before facing Motherwell in the final before a capacity crowd of 132,000. Bobby had played in every game and duly earned his first major honour playing for Celtic.

Celtic XI *v.* Motherwell, Scottish Cup final: Hunter, Fallon, Rollo, Evans, Boden, Baillee, Weir, Collins, McPhail, Peacock, Tully.

Celtic and Lazio prepare for a not so 'friendly' encounter in Rome.

Celtic XI *v.* Morton, September 1950. *From left to right, back row:* Haughney, Milne, Bonner, Evans, McGrory, Bailee, McGrory (manager). *Front row:* Collins, Fernie, McPhail, Peacock, Tully.

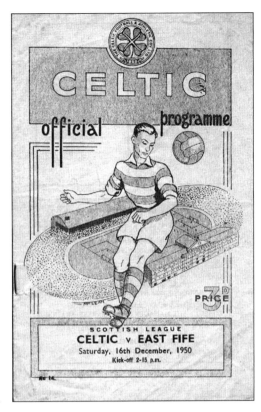

Hat-trick hero.

Throughout the build-up Celtic had one major fitness doubt, John McPhail, and it was touch and go if he would make the final. In the end he took his place in the side and would come up trumps with the winning goal. Bobby recalled the goal on 13 minutes after the game:

Joe Baillee began the move when he dispossessed Motherwell's Wilson Humphries in our half before sending a deep ball down the middle. John McPhail picked up the ball and beat Andy Paton then headed towards goal with Willie Kilmarnock and Archie Shaw in pursuit. Their 'keeper, John Johnston, rushed out to block him but with both backs getting closer John lobbed the ball neatly over the goalie's head and into the net. His run was timed so well that he didn't even break his stride.

At the final whistle the scenes were just incredible. Our supporters in Hampden's Rutherglen End went crazy; throwing their scarves, flags and banners in the air. Everyone was hugging each other, they were just so happy and the cheers went on for ages. There was so much relief not only for supporters but also from the players.

The victory was a major achievement historically for Celtic because apart from being the youngest team ever in the club's history to win a major trophy, this was Celtic's first honour since 1938. The team had been inconsistent for some time, but at last they had put together a series of results for a memorable victory.

23

Hampden here we come.

Celtic win the Cup.

During the close season, Bobby was a member of the Celtic squad that travelled to America on the *Queen Mary*. Bobby recalled:

I could barely believe it; I'd hardly travelled further than Rothesay at the time. The ship was gigantic and more than once I had to ask for directions back to my cabin! Jimmy McGrory quickly became the most popular person on board when he filled the Cup with champagne and took it around the decks for the passengers.

As usual Charlie Tully was at the centre of the pranks, he even hid the cup from Jimmy on one occasion. His joke at a reception before our clash with New York All-Stars almost backfired when the bag he had hidden it in went missing, but it turned up shortly afterwards with the rest of our baggage. He was pretty relieved, but it didn't stop his antics.

On Celtic's return, the team was greeted by 15,000 supporters at Glasgow Central Station. The reception was unprecedented and the players had to be protected by police.

To cap a memorable season, on the international front, after pulling out of a clash against Switzerland due to injury, Bobby made his full Scotland debut against Wales in Cardiff on 21 October 1950. One of a number of players to be called up late for the clash, Bobby provided the cross for a spectacular flying header from Billy Liddell after Lawrie Reilly had scored twice. Liddell's goal settled the match and ensured a winning start for Scotland's latest cap.

Davie Collins recalled fondly his brother's international bow: 'When Bobby joined Celtic, I became a staunch supporter. Celtic supporters loved Bobby. He may have been small, but he played his heart out and always played to win. It was just a matter of time

Right: Bobby puts a shine on the Scottish Cup.

Below: Relaxing on the *Queen Mary*.

Left: Bobby and Charlie Tully show off the cup to American supporters.

Below: Class of 1950/51 arrives in the United States.

Scotland debut.

before he made the Scottish team; the papers were full of snippets. The whole family was so proud when he was called up for the Wales match. I travelled to Cardiff on the overnight train with dad, Uncle John and Tommy McGrotty. We won and Bobby had a great game. It was the first of many great memories of his international career.'

The 3-1 victory saw Bobby selected for the next 2 games, both at Hampden Park. His home bow could not have gone better as Northern Ireland were put to the sword 6-1; Billy Steel scoring four goals. The clash against Austria, played on a frozen pitch, however ended in a disappointing 1-0 defeat.

The loss meant that Scotland were the first 'home' international team to be beaten on their own soil by foreign opposition and it raised questions about Scotland's standing in the world game. As selectors pondered their best formation, Bobby was dropped from the side and would not win another full cap for four years, although he would remain a regular in the Scottish League representative XI.

I was disappointed to be dropped but I was young and knew I'd get another chance. The association's secretary George Graham organised everything and would be 'manager' by the time I made my debut.

The 1951/52 season began with the Festival of Britain programme and Celtic took part in the St Mungo Cup competition. Playing before capacity crowds, Celtic overcame Hearts, Clyde (after drawing the first match 4-4) and Raith Rovers to face Aberdeen in the final. Bobby recalled in a column:

The clash with Clyde was particularly memorable for me because I grabbed two goals and we came from two goals behind twice to force a replay, which we won with something to spare.

In the final at Hampden Park, before 81,000 spectators, Celtic again fell two goals behind, before Charlie Tully won a corner just before the interval after playing a throw-in off a defender's back! From Tully's centre, Sean Fallon scored.

Celtic dominated the second half. Fallon notched an equalizer before Jimmy Walsh scored a controversial winner twenty minutes from time after Tully had appeared to drag the ball back from behind the dead-ball line prior to crossing for Walsh's strike. The referee consulted his linesman but the goal stood. Celtic had won the cup for the only time it was competed for.

When the real action began, Celtic struggled for consistency and for two seasons ended the League campaign in mid-table as Hibernian and Rangers claimed another title each. Bobby top-scored in all competitions for the only time as a Celtic player with 13 goals, but grabbed only 3 goals the following term, a season when he missed the opening three months of the campaign due to an injury that limited his appearances to just 19 games.

On the domestic cup front, Rangers ended Celtic's League Cup and Scottish Cup hopes. The latter tournament saw an incredible tie in February 1953 when Celtic were drawn at Falkirk in the third round. The match has gone down into club folklore following the performance of the mercurial Charlie Tully. Home supporters were hoping for a cup upset with Celtic lying in mid-table, and early on their hopes were high with Falkirk two goals ahead. The second half though saw Celtic in determined mood and they got their reward when Tully scored direct from a left-wing corner at the Railway End of the narrow Brockville pitch. Supporters went wild, but their joy was tempered when the goal was disallowed as the ball was adjudged not to be in the quarter-circle. Undaunted, Tully replaced the

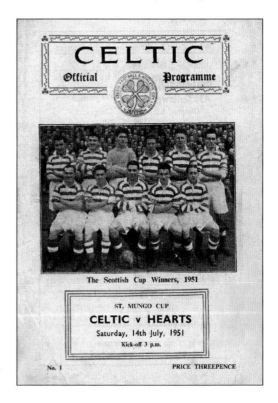

Another trophy claimed, the St Mungo Cup.

Bobby in action, *c.* 1953.

ball and promptly struck another sweet corner directly into the net to the delight of his adoring fans. After the pitch was cleared, Fernie levelled the scores prior to McGrory striking the winner with a terrific strike from 20 yards. Again fans invaded the pitch.

The star was undoubtedly Charlie, who in the dying moments dribbled towards his own goal before winning a goal kick off an opposing attacker! Charlie was some player. His display against Falkirk was incredible, and what could one say about his goal direct from a corner? It was typical Charlie. In the quarter-finals we were a shade unlucky against Rangers because I struck a post and had another effort saved on the line. Charlie also went close before they grabbed a late goal to clinch victory. It was a bitter disappointment.

To mark the ascension to the throne of Queen Elizabeth II, Bobby played in the Coronation Cup. Eight teams took part in the tournament from England and Scotland: Aberdeen, Arsenal, Celtic, Hibernian, Manchester United, Newcastle United, Rangers and Tottenham Hotspur. Scoring the only goal of the clash against Arsenal direct from a corner in the opening round, Bobby helped defeat Manchester United in the semi-final before helping Celtic triumph 2-0 over Hibernian in the final. Celtic were by far the best team in the competition and deserved to win.

So close.

By now Celtic had a new skipper, who would become a legend. Jock Stein, who took over the captaincy from John McPhail during the 1952/53 season, joined Celtic in December 1951, but his arrival from Albion Rovers was not welcomed unanimously by supporters. Bobby recalled in a newspaper interview.

Some supporters threatened to boycott games if he was selected, which was incredible. Jock may have been turning professional at the age of twenty-eight, but you had to give him a chance. Fortunately the manager did give him an opportunity and Jock soon settled into the team.

Jimmy Gribben was instrumental in bringing the Big Man to Parkhead and what a decision that would prove to be, not only during my time as a player but also in the long-term history of the club. The successes he would ultimately guide them to would be quite extraordinary.

At the time Jimmy was assistant trainer and Jock was playing in Wales. When Jock suffered a couple of burglaries at his home in Burnbank, Jimmy helped him sort things out domestically and reminded Celtic chairman Bob Kelly of how well Jock had played against Celtic the previous season when he was an Albion Rovers player. Before long he was duly signed and it has to be the best signing the club has ever made.

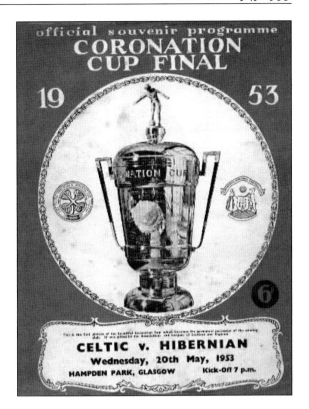

Right: Royal honours.

Below: Coronation Cup winners led by skipper Jock Stein. Bobby is extreme left on front row.

31

Jock read the game well; could spot danger and opportunities quickly and as a player we all respected him, but it was as a captain that you really saw his credentials. He was always encouraging and demanded more effort, and got it. Nobody escaped praise when it was warranted or a sharp word when necessary.

My early years at the club had been terrific. We may not have been successful every season, but there was nothing like playing for your home-town club and the support we received was something else. There was great camaraderie in the team and despite winning only one major trophy we believed that more success was just around the corner.

THREE

JUST CHAMPION AND
TRIPLE CUP HEARTBREAK
1953-1956

The 1953/54 campaign did not begin brightly for Celtic. Knocked out of the League Cup in the early phases, they won only one of their opening three League matches. Slowly but surely though, Celtic began to string results together and moved up the table into a challenging position. Bobby was playing well and after grabbing the only goal against Clyde for Celtic's first win of the campaign, one match proved particularly memorable as he joined a rare breed of players to score a hat-trick of penalties in a match; against Aberdeen in the League clash on 26 September 1953.

Following the game, Aberdeen's right-back, Jimmy Mitchell, was not downhearted despite the fact that all three penalties had been awarded against him by referee Mr A. McEwan. He told reporters: 'I was mad at the time, but I am not the least bit annoyed about it now. If they had been penalties I would have been downhearted, but they weren't. They were farcical.'

Destiny awaits.

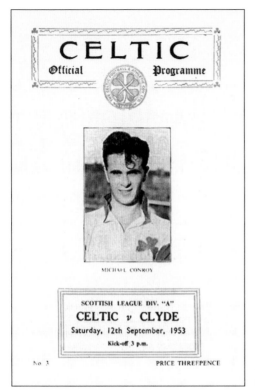

Bobby's winner earns Celtic a first League win.

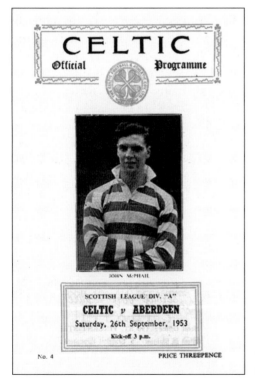

Treble chance! Bobby grabs three penalties.

Happy New Year.

With Jock Stein a calming influence in defence, Celtic were becoming difficult opponents to beat and a 2-0 win over Rangers on New Year's Day moved Celtic closer to top-of-the-table Hearts. When the two sides clashed at Tynecastle during February, the home side's 3-2 win appeared to have settled the destiny of the title with Hearts now 7 points clear, even though Celtic had 3 games in hand. Suddenly though, Hearts began to falter and nine consecutive victories sensationally brought the title to Celtic Park. The purple patch saw Celtic defeat Dundee 5-1, East Fife 4-1, Airdrie 6-0, Partick Thistle 3-1, Stirling Albion 4-0, St Mirren 3-1, Falkirk 3-0, Hibernian 3-0 and Hamilton Academicals 1-0. Finishing 5 points ahead of Hearts, it was an amazing turnaround that stunned pundits and sent Celtic supporters delirious. Their first crown since the 1937/38 campaign, it would be their only title for 28 years until Jock Stein began his reign of success as manager.

Celtic: P-30 W-24 D-1 L-5 F-73 A-26 Pts-49

Appearances: Bell 7, Boden 9, Bonnar 22, Collins 20, Conroy 2, Evans 30, Fallon 20, Fernie 23, Haughney 30, Higgins 14, McMahon 1, McPhail 4, Meechan 18, Mochan 17, Peacock 29, Reid 3, Rowan 1, Smith 3, Stein 28, Tully 21, Walsh 28

Goalscorers: Walsh 19, Fernie 12, Higgins 9, Mochan 9, Haughney 7, Collins 5, Tully 4, McPhail 2, Boden 2, Smith 1, Evans 1, Reid 1, Rowan 1, Stein 1 OG 2

Bobby in action against Airdrie as Celtic hit six.

Bobby had missed just five League encounters, but an injury against Hearts cost him the chance of claiming another Scottish Cup winner's medal as Celtic clinched a League and cup double for the first time in forty years. He played in the opening three rounds against Falkirk, Stirling Albion and Hamilton Academicals but missed the semi-final win over Motherwell, after a replay, and the victory over Aberdeen in the final when Sean Fallon grabbed the winning goal.

It was a fairytale end of the season for Fallon, who missed the majority of the campaign, but came back into the frame during the title run-in. Scoring 5 goals in the last 7 League games, Fallon capped the season with a goal in the cup final.

It was really disappointing to miss out on the cup final, but I was delighted for the lads. I'd been out injured for around ten weeks, but after battling back to fitness I'd hoped to be in contention. It wasn't to be though, and I couldn't complain because the team had played well and reached the final without me. I had to wait for my chance to get back into the first XI. I was just delighted to play and score in the final League game two days after the cup final and enjoyed all the celebrations. Our fans were ecstatic.

It was a wonderful achievement because the team had been inconsistent for a number of years so it was fantastic to put a run together. Overcoming Hearts was a great effort by the squad.

As defending Champions, Celtic began the final sixteen-club League campaign in 1954/55 in fine style, winning 4 of their opening 5 matches, however only 2 victories in their next 7 games would prove crucial. Despite losing just one League game before New Year and two after, Celtic had to settle for the runners-up spot behind Aberdeen. Finishing 3 points adrift of the Dons, Celtic could hardly have done more to retain their crown. They lost two fewer games than Aberdeen and finished with a flourish after losing 4-1 at Rangers on New Year's Day; winning 11 out of 14 matches. Too many drawn games was the deciding factor (Celtic 8 Aberdeen 1).

Celtic did have the satisfaction of gaining three more points than in the Championship season and their total of 46 would have been sufficient to win the title the two seasons prior to that.

The Champions depart on a post-season tour.

Bobby shows his golfing skills at Turnberry, July 1954.

Of course it was disappointing because we had been consistent. You had to hand it to Aberdeen though, they were worthy winners.

In the Scottish Cup, once again Celtic reached the final after defeating Alloa, Kilmarnock, Hamilton Academicals and Airdrie. Bobby played in every match but a reckless challenge in the final on Clyde's goalkeeper during a 1-1 draw saw him dropped for the replay by Celtic chairman Robert Kelly. Celtic missed Bobby's tenacity and Clyde's 1-0 victory meant that Celtic had gone from double-winners to double losers.

It was really disappointing. I wonder in the modern game how many chairmen would have taken that decision. I was not happy.

On a far brighter note Beryl and Bobby Collins celebrated the birth of their son Robert in October 1954 and after four years in the international wilderness Bobby was recalled to the Scottish side. In the intervening years, his country had endured mixed fortunes and their recent form had seen two humiliating defeats, a 7-0 thumping at the hands of Uruguay in the World Cup finals and an embarrassing 7-2 defeat against England during the 1954/55 Home International Championships.

The defeat at Wembley in April 1955 was the last straw for selectors, who made nine changes against Portugal; the only home game of four post-season matches. A 3-0 win justified their selection policy. With tough fixtures planned against Yugoslavia, Austria and Hungary, Bobby returned to the side in their first fixture in Belgrade. In a battling display the Scots twice came from behind to draw 2-2 against Yugoslavia and were somewhat unfortunate not to win when they were denied a last-minute penalty. Four days later national pride was restored after a thumping 4-1 win in Vienna.

Played four days after Austria had gained full independence, after concluding a peace state treaty with wartime occupying powers, the atmosphere was hostile throughout. Scotland controlled the match for long periods, scoring in the opening and closing minutes of the game. Clearly frustrated, and no doubt in mind of the historical importance, home players engaged in fistfights throughout the game, and twice hundreds of fans invaded the pitch. The only surprise was that only one Austrian player was sent off, Barschandt, for persistent fouls on Scotland captain Gordon Smith. Smith was escorted off the field at the end by police, as was the Scottish team coach when they left the ground. The following morning Scottish papers were full of praise.

Alec Young of the *Scottish Daily Mail* wrote: 'This was a great Scottish victory. No team has been asked to do more and no team has made such a magnificent response

Back in action, 1954.

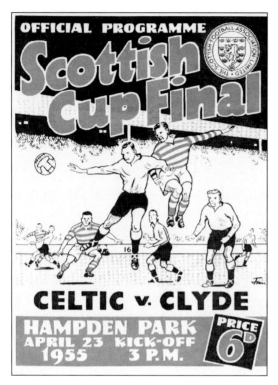

Cup heartbreak as
Bobby is dropped for
the replay.

as our lads did in this amazing 'Battle of Prater Stadium'. In the midst of all the excitement of this clash it was a matter of light relief to see Bobby Collins, a lion-heart terrier, repeatedly being pushed aside, yet repeatedly coming back again and even squaring up to six-footers when as often happened football science was forsaken for the fistic arts.'

Tommy Muirhead commented in the *Scottish Daily Express*: 'The day we have longed for has come at last. The day the Hungarians, recognised as the world's best footballers, admit they are scared of meeting Scotland. That is what their representatives told me here tonight after we had thrashed an Austrian team who stopped at nothing in an attempt to hold us.'

Hugh Taylor observed in the *Evening Citizen*: 'The Austrian footballers, you can give the name to athletes who would have been a match for Marciano and Cockell combined, had forgotten their peace treaty had been signed. They kicked, pushed and barged. They tore through the air at our boys with the speed of the men on the flying trapeze we had seen at the circus the night before. They clicked heels, whipped pins and punched as though they were posing for a film called "The Referee's Nightmare". It was unbelievable.'

The final clash of the tour saw the Hungarians overturn a half-time deficit to win 3-1 after Gordon Smith had scored just before the break. The result could have been very different had Billy Liddell not blazed a penalty wide and struck the woodwork twice.

On the march! Scotland's squad enjoys a stroll in Austria.

The 1955 post-season tour was a resounding success for the Scots and Bobby Collins had made a major impact. Off the field, Scottish administrators were discussing numerous issues including Under-23 and 'B' international teams, trial games, selection policy, more pre-match sessions and most importantly a full-time manager. Times were changing and Bobby was beginning to cement his place in the side as the team developed for the World Cup finals in 1958.

Dedication had been the key for Bobby, a point not forgotten by his great friend Tommy McGrotty. 'I was with him the night before his Celtic debut and he just took it took it in his stride. He was determined to succeed. After playing a few games for his country he was disappointed to be out of the international frame, but I knew he'd be back because he was so disciplined and strict with his fitness. He would not go out after a Wednesday, and on New Year's Eve he'd go to bed at 7 p.m. At midnight he'd get up for a few moments then went back to bed. He was thrilled to be recalled.'

It was wonderful to be back and part of a really successful tour, which gave us tremendous confidence for the battles ahead. George Graham was a disciplinarian but he also recognised that we had to unwind when a tour was over. Our tour had gone well and on the last night we were staying at Plaza Hotel in Zurich. The team was in high spirits and the manager turned a blind eye to Tommy Docherty and Alex Young's antics when they proceeded to swap around guests' shoes outside their rooms waiting to be cleaned. George was firm but also sensible in his managerial approach.

No real harm was done and the perpetrators went unpunished. I couldn't wait for our next match.

In 1955/56 the Scottish League was increased to eighteen clubs. Celtic began slowly, but 9 wins in an 11-match unbeaten run pushed them into contention by the turn of the year. Unfortunately just 5 victories in the second half of the season saw them finish fifth behind Champions Rangers. In the League Cup they failed to get past the qualifying stages for the fourth consecutive season; however the cup run was notable for a sensational 4-1 win at Ibrox when Bobby Collins had been in imperious form.

Harry Andrew of the *Scottish Sunday Express* wrote: 'Little Bobby promptly became the big man of this game, wreaking havoc with the Rangers defence in a multitude of ways. His name isn't on the scoresheet but his influence was apparent in every minute of the ninety.'

Esteemed journalist Jack Harkness of the *Sunday Post* said that it had been fifty years since Celtic had run Rangers so ragged and stated that it would take another fifty years before another 'Old Firm' battle was so one-sided. Harkness would review his thoughts after the 1957 League Cup final!

In the Scottish Cup, Celtic made it all the way to the final after defeating Morton, Ayr United, Airdrie and Clyde. For Bobby, who had scored in the opening three rounds, the win over cup-holders Clyde was sweet, but for the third year in succession he would miss out on the big day, following a knee injury sustained in the last minute of a 3-1

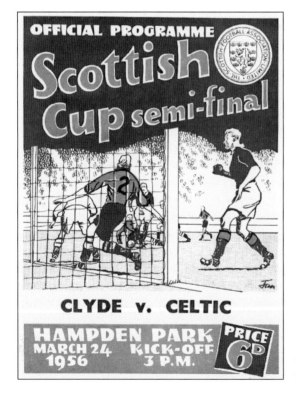

Celtic win but the cup
final hoodoo strikes again.

OFFICIAL PROGRAMME

RANGERS versus CELTIC

6d

GLASGOW CUP FINAL REPLAY
at HAMPDEN PARK
MONDAY, 26th DECEMBER, —1955

KICK-OFF
1.45 p.m.

Bobby's brace secures a
memorable 'Old Firm' triumph.

League win over Airdrie four days after the semi-final triumph. Celtic's 3-1 defeat to
Hearts in the subsequent final was galling for all concerned.

*I could barely believe it when I was ruled out of a major final for the third year
running. Losing was bad enough; sitting on the sidelines unable to help made it even
more frustrating.*

Domestically, the campaign had ended disappointingly, but supporters had seen the
team win the Glasgow Cup during the opening months of the 1955/56 season.
Incredibly, since Bobby had turned professional, he had never been on the winning
side, though twice, against Partick Thistle and Clyde, he had received runners-up
medals. All this changed following victories over Partick and Clyde in the opening
rounds. The final saw Celtic take on Rangers in front of 53,000 fans. A 1-1 draw meant
a replay at Hampden, which attracted a bumper attendance. In a fluctuating game,
Rangers opened the scoring on 22 minutes only for Celtic to reply moments later. Then
Celtic took the lead before Rangers equalized just on the interval. Celtic's third goal on
the hour lasted less than a minute before two quick-fire goals in the last six minutes
settled a pulsating match. Bobby grabbed a brace, including the all-important fourth
goal.

Waverley of the *Daily Record* wrote: 'Lively, exhilarating and all the time endowed
with uncertainty. It was a game of continually changing fortune, right up to the end
when, to borrow a phrase from boxing, Celtic produced a one-two punch. It came in

the form of goals from Collins and Fernie; a punch that put Rangers out for the count.'

Matches against Rangers were always eagerly anticipated by players and fans alike. They could be brutal battles though. Indeed, Jock Stein's career would ultimately end following a bad ankle injury sustained during the season in one such 'Old Firm' match. In his regular Saturday *Evening Times* weekly newspaper column, 'The Bobby Collins Corner', Bobby gave his thoughts on the world famous fixture. (*c.* 1955)

When a young player signs on the dotted line for Rangers or Celtic there should be a clause in the contract agreeing to pay him 'danger money'. Maybe you should ask for the cruet and take the 'danger money' line with just the teeniest pinch of salt, but you know, it is tough, really tough, when you are playing at the top and playing for one of the halves of the 'Old Firm'.

I am not suggesting for a split second that all the other boys in Scottish football go out to cripple the Rangers and Celtic players when they come up against us. Of course they don't, but they do play harder than usual, and they do tackle harder than usual whenever they meet.

It is quite a feat to come off the field with a victory over a colour scheme made up of light blue or green and white, and I know for a fact the half-time pep talk in quite a few dressing rooms consists of the order "Go out and get tore into this lot".

Believe me they do get tore in. The result is that almost every game for Rangers and Celtic is a cup-tie affair, and we have to keep going all out for the ninety minutes to make sure there is no slip-up in the final result, and if you are playing that type of football week in and week out the risk of injury increases in proportion.

Take a look at the present season and the Celtic casualty list. Tully, Fernie, Fallon, Walsh, Higgins and Stein are only a few who have been out of the game all inside of five weeks. We have been literally queuing up for a place on Mr Dowdell's table, and exactly the same sort of thing happened over at Ibrox last year.

Although I know full well that injuries come at one time or another to all players, I am willing to take a small wager which says that over any season Rangers and Celtic will top the Division A casualty list. I repeat that we are not the victims of dirty play, although the ball player does come in for more than his fair share of crude tackling, but if you are pounding away every Saturday in life, and in midweek too, you are almost bound to pull a muscle or maybe tear a cartilage.

On the international scene, Bobby's knee injury meant that he missed out on Scotland's post-season fixtures, although he had taken part in the first quadruple tie in the history of the Home International Championships since its inception in 1883/84 as goal average was not accepted as a deciding factor.

There was no questioning the best performance, which saw Scotland defeat Wales 2-0. The Scottish forward line of Gordon Smith, Bobby Johnstone, Laurie Reilly, Bobby Collins and Jackie Henderson combined as smoothly as any British side of the previous decade according to experts and only a brilliant display by Jack Kelsey kept the score down, Johnstone scoring a brace. John Charles had no answer for the Welsh as Scots

High jinks... Bobby and Willie Fernie warm up before a big clash.

Above: Bobby goes close for Scotland.

Opposite: Hitching a ride from big George Young.

skipper George Young kept him at bay. The victory made up for a disappointing 2-1 defeat against Northern Ireland and set them up for their clash with the 'auld enemy, a match that could have settled the championships.

Sadly, injury meant Bobby missed out against England. Scotland seemed set to record a win at Hampden Park for the first time since 1937 after Graham Leggat opened the scoring. It was not to be however, as two minutes from time Johnny Haynes converted Roger Byrne's centre for a controversial equalizer to silence the crowd and deny the Scots an outright title.

Missing out on a second cup final was again a big disappointment as was missing out on the clash against England, which would have been my first against the 'auld enemy. I'd have loved to pit myself against the likes of Stanley Matthews and co. Nevertheless I'd become a regular in the side and had the World Cup qualifying matches to look forward to.

FOUR

UP FOR THE CUPS
1956-1957

A broken leg sustained in a League clash at Dundee meant that Bobby missed three months of the season as for the second year running Celtic ended the campaign behind the pack in fifth place; Rangers retained their crown. Prior to his injury though, he had helped Celtic ease through the League Cup knockout stages for only the third time

Agony at Dens Park…a broken leg against Dundee.

Celtic win on aggregate.

since its inception. They would go all the way to the final after overcoming Aberdeen, Rangers and East Fife in the qualifying section, Dunfermline 6-3 on aggregate in the quarter-finals and Clyde 2-0 in a fine semi-final. Bobby had played in every game and would not miss out on a major final as in previous seasons.

Celtic XI *v.* Partick Thistle, Scottish League Cup final: Beattie, Haughney, Fallon, Evans, Jack, Peacock, Tully, Collins, McPhail, Fernie, Mochan

Following a 0-0 draw Celtic won the replay 3-0, McPhail grabbing a brace before Bobby sealed victory with his only goal in a major cup final.

I was naturally delighted. Having missed out on other finals, it was great to make it and I was also able to complete my set of domestic honours.

In the Scottish Cup, Celtic made progress after defeating Forres Mechs, Rangers, after a titanic 4-4 draw, and St Mirren, before losing out in the semi-finals against Kilmarnock. The clash against Rangers is still regarded as one of the most exciting ever. Building up a 4-2 lead, Bobby grabbing the third with a brilliant hooked shot, with a few minutes to go, Bob MacNab of *The People* said it was a 1000-1 certainty that Celtic would win: 'There will never be another match like it... not for brilliant individuals, but for the sheer desperate excitement of it all, for the gameness of two sides who flatly refused to quit and for the agonising urgency of the last 15 minutes.'

Stalemate but Celtic win the replay.

No cup double as Celtic lose 3-1.

During the season, prior to Scotland taking on Spain and Switzerland in World Cup qualifying fixtures, Bobby played against the Irish League and scored for the Scottish League in a 4-2 win against a Football League XI. Gair Henderson of the *Evening Times* wrote: 'For Collins the match was the greatest triumph of his career. His speed was a killing weapon against Sillett and Edwards, his shooting was deadly and smack on target, and his trickery on the ball must have been an inspiration to every other member of the team. Undoubtedly Bobby's best.'

Waverley of the *Daily Record* felt: 'In the Scots' most deserved victory Collins was the outstanding personality of the match. Repeatedly his skill, enterprise and tremendous shooting power raised the 70,000 crowd to the highest pitch of excitement. How they enjoyed the brilliance of this little fellow!'

The most entertaining clash of the Home Internationals was Scotland's 2-2 draw with Wales. The match, in which Welsh legend Trevor Ford played his last game, saw the home side build up a two-goal lead, with John Charles and Ray Daniel dictating play. The Scots forward line included Celtic duo Collins and Fernie on the left wing. They eventually made their presence felt and engineered a share of the spoils with two goals in the last six minutes.

Bobby missed a 1-0 victory over Ireland, a match marred by a bad injury to Doug Cowie, but was back in the side against England at Wembley. The game got off to a great start for the Tartan Army as Tommy Ring scored in the first minute, but debutant Derek Kevan equalized before Duncan Edwards secured victory with a stunning 25-yard

Scottish League XI *v.* Irish League, 1956.

Scotland XI *v.* Wales, October 1956. *From left to right, back row:* Parker, McColl, Younger, Hewie, Cowie. *Front row:* Leggat, Mudie, Reilly, Young, Collins, Fernie.

strike seven minutes from time. W. Capel Kirby of the *Empire News and Sunday Chronicle* commented: 'Scotland were made to look a great deal better than they really were by an England forward line which never worked in unison. As for Scotland… the only danger man was Bobby Collins, who was always looking for the half-chance and was speedy in getting into position.'

It was in this clash that I faced the great Stanley Matthews. He may not have been at his brilliant best but he was for me the best player I ever faced. Stan had it all. He could beat you on the outside or on the inside. He would tie a player in knots, before delivering the most wicked of crosses from the byline. He was a phenomenal player and it was an honour to be on the same field as him. Mind you there were other class players in Tom Finney, Billy Wright and Duncan Edwards. It was wonderful taking on such stars.

Within a month Collins and co. consigned the result to the history books following their most stirring post-war performance; a sensational 4-2 victory against Spain in their opening World Cup clash at Hampden. Every player was a hero, but overcoming blatant obstruction tactics Jackie Mudie, Tommy Ring and Bobby were the star performers. Mudie won the headlines following a classy hat-trick against a star-studded Spanish team that included the legendary Alfredo di Stefano in their ranks. The victory was the start of a superb post-season tour, which saw the Scots come from behind to defeat Switzerland 2-1 in their second World Cup fixture; Bobby notching the winner on 72 minutes. Just two points from their return fixtures would settle the Scots' passage to the World Cup finals.

Waverley wrote in the *Daily Record*: 'The Scots were the more solid lot, survived the opening flashes of the opposition, were a shade fortunate to do so, and then went on to deserve their victory.' Regarding the winning goal Waverley noted: 'The Swiss shied off the tackle because they were tired and our fellows were given plenty of room to operate. Such tactics were almost certain to be punished and punished they were. Smith forced a corner and took it himself. Bobby was left on his own to step in, jump high and head the ball down and past Parlier with not a Swiss player making any attempt to impede him.'

Douglas Ritchie of the *Daily Herald* wrote: 'Scotland can thank their mighty midgets for this victory. I give you Jackie Mudie and Bobby Collins the lionhearts. They got Scotland's goals, both from headers and both from corners. It was fantastic as neither of this pair can draw himself above the 5ft 5in mark even with long studs, but they were the big men in the Scots attack.'

Buoyed by their success, the players proved it was no freak result when they defeated West Germany 3-1, Bobby scoring twice against the defending World Champions. This was Scotland's first win in Germany and Bobby's best display in a Scottish jersey. Commenting on Bobby's brace Douglas Ritchie wrote: 'Scott and Ring 'sizzled' the ball from wing to wing and the outside left turned his final cross low in front of goal. Szymaniak slipped going to clear and Collins darted in to score. Collins struck again after 56 minutes. The wee Scot waltzed past a defender and sent in an atomic shot that almost ripped the roof of the net. The tiny knot of sore-throated Scots in the vast crowd loved that one and even the Germans couldn't help cheering.'

The final goal made headline news. *The Bulletin* commented: 'Collins picked up a ball 25 yards out, surveyed the landscape, saw nobody in better position, and immediately smashed the ball into the roof of the net. The German goalkeeper was dumbfounded, the other players heartbroken, and the crowd astonished, at the power which came from the foot of the smallest man on the field.'

Two of the best goals that I ever scored came in this match. Jackie Mudie set me up for the first; as for the second, that was a result of a throw-in routine I had with Tommy Docherty. It worked to perfection and I hit an absolute screamer.

Scotland duly lost 4-1 in Madrid but it failed to dampen the squad's spirit as their destiny was still in their hands. Bobby was now a national star and began to feature prominently in football articles and annuals of the era. In a newspaper article about his diet, Bobby explained his blueprint for energy was to keep himself 'breezy, bouncing and bustin' to go'. The reporter noted: 'Collins has got a shot that for sheer power rivals Charlie Fleming's cannonball finishing and in any conditions he is always going as strongly after 90 minutes as he was at the start.' Bobby said:

It's a combination of several things I suppose. First, there's the food I eat. During the week I can have a steak every day if I want to, and I often do. It's part of the four-course lunch provided by the club at a Glasgow restaurant. I usually have tomato juice, soup, meat and a sweet, practically everything except tea or coffee, which I lay off at lunchtime, though I have them at other meals at home. Before a game I stick to poached eggs, toast, orange juice and a glucose drink. At half-time I always have orange juice, very rarely any tea and only a mouthful on a cold day.

Training…I do a special series of short sprints designed to get me quicker off my mark. If you can get to the ball first you'll conserve energy by not having to do much chasing, but I haven't required much training these past few weeks. With 2 games a week it's not necessary.

Apart from eating and training though, there's only one thing that keeps me going. That's the spirit at Celtic Park. Of course I feel it all the more because the club have treated me so well in helping me get over my arm injury and giving me a chance to come back.

In the 1957 *Big Book of Football Champions*, Bobby appeared in a series called 'Portrait of a Champion'. *The Plucky One* chronicled his career to date.

'There is an old Scottish saying "Guid gear goes intae sma' bulk". It is true of Celtic's sturdy, compact forward, Bobby Collins, who reaches five feet four inches when he stretches to his toes.

'What makes a great footballer? Courage: Twice bad injuries cost Collins international caps and last year he was out of action for four months with a broken leg. Yet he never shirks a tackle and can rough a passage with the best. Versatility: He has played three times for the Scottish League…at outside right, inside right and outside right, and scored a goal in each. Assurance: Look at the cheeky impudence with which he rounds a back to have a crack at goal.

'Collins' size four boots are among the smallest in first-class soccer. Yet they pack an astonishingly hard shot. His energy, speed and pluck are also out of proportion to his size and his ball control and craft are excellent. His greatest asset is self-confidence.

'Since the war, Scotland have relied too much on long passing, physique and vigour, instead of deftness, positioning and finesse. In the main, as a result, big and strong players have held sway.

'The Scottish tradition in soccer is that the ball should be kept on the ground, where it belongs. That gives the little fellow an equal chance with opponents who tower five or six inches above them.

'Some of the biggest names in Scottish football are men great in ability though small in stature. Such are Bobby Steel, Alex James, the 'wee blue devil' Alan Morton, Hughie Gallagher, Jimmy McMullan and George Brown. Celtic's manager Jimmy McGrory set

George Young introduces his team to Lord Roseberry before a clash against the Auld Enemy, 1957.

World Cup hero... Bobby's goal beats the Swiss.

up an all-time career record by scoring 550 goals in first-class soccer with Celtic. He too is on the small side.

'Bobby Collins is a worthy descendant of this line. His rise shows that Scottish football is returning to the old sense of values.'

Things could hardly be going better for me. I was playing with confidence and knew that the coming season would be memorable.

FIVE

SEVEN PAST NIVEN
1957-1958

The League campaign began with Celtic winning 8 of their opening 11 League fixtures. Among a number of terrific displays was a 3-2 win at Ibrox, Celtic's first in the League for twenty-one years. Bobby opened the scoring with a terrific solo goal on 19 minutes.

Charles Shankland observed in the *Sunday Pictorial*: 'Now this was the real 'Old Firm' stuff. None of the namby-pamby 'after-you' milk-and-water soccer, that's the sort that has been masquerading at Rangers-Celtic football for the past few seasons, but not yesterday. Sure there were fouls, plenty of them, but nothing that was really dirty. Like anyone else I'll condemn dirty play and have done so in any team or player, but here was the old Rangers-Celtic 'needle' played in he-man style. Wee Bobby Collins was right on top. Like a little green-and-white-striped wasp, he buzzed in, through and around the Rangers defence, and he carried plenty of sting with him too.'

A challenge seemed on the cards, but four successive defeats at the turn of the year put paid their title hopes. Five wins in the last seven fixtures saw Celtic claim third spot, 16 points behind Hearts.

Despite an early exit in the Scottish Cup, the season did not end without success. Celtic's defence of the League Cup began well as they overcame with ease Airdrie, East Fife and Hibernian in the qualifiers. Bobby grabbed 3 of Celtic's 18 goals, and a treble helped defeat Third Lanark in the quarter-finals. Another strike against Clyde proved decisive in a hard-fought 4-2 win in the semi-finals. The result meant that Rangers and Celtic would contest the first 'Old Firm' final for twenty-nine years. Bobby was Man of the Match.

Harry Andrew wrote of Celtic's victory in the *Scottish Sunday Express*: 'Bobby didn't have just one inspired moment, he had a dozen and four of them produced goals. He was the one forward of all ten who combined energy, subtlety, ball control, accuracy in the pass and a finishing punch. And his goal was the most spectacular, the most timely that can ever have come Celtic's way in a cup tie. There they were, these Celts, back on their heels with 10 minutes of the second half gone, stunned by the knowledge that a comfortable two-goal lead had suddenly vanished. Then Collins changed the whole picture. He took the ball away on his own, steadied some 30 yards out and hit a tremendous drive. Goalkeeper McCulloch watched it roar towards, and apparently past, his right-hand post. At the last moment, the ball swerved inside the post and up into the roof of the net. The goalkeeper still hadn't moved. An amazing, breathtaking

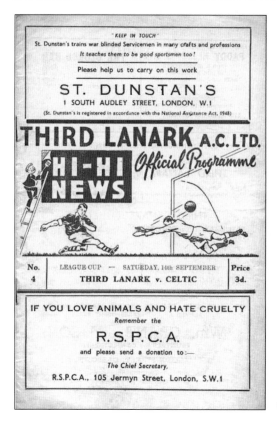

One step to Hampden.

goal, but don't call it a fluke, I've seen Bobby hit those 'swerves' too often. Oh yes, Celtic deserved to win. No argument about it.'

Gair Henderson made these comments in the *Evening Times*: 'Collins for the past two years has been the most profitable football player in Scotland, and the Celtic supporters are rightly convinced that to Parkhead he is worth his weight in gold. Apart from his tremendous rocket-shot from 25 yards which left young McCulloch rooted to his goal line, Bobby had a hand in the three other Celtic goals. But what I liked most was the example he set to his team in enthusiasm and mobility. Just after Innes had pulled back Clyde from 2-0 down to 2-2, Collins was back defending furiously on his own six-yard line. From there he slipped the ball to Donnelly and instead of saying "Well that's my job done", the wee one raced as hard as his legs could carry him to the halfway line and started up the attack which was the forerunner of his own magnificent goal.'

Jack Harkness enthused in the *Sunday Post*: 'Here we had a humdinger of a cup-tie, plus half a dozen humdinger goals, plus plenty of thrills and spills and excitement, and the only difference between the two teams were a mere sixty-three inches; the sixty-three inches that go to make up Bobby Collins. Early on, when Celtic sorely needed a goal to settle them, Bobby took it on himself to lay on a couple. Back came this shock team of Shawfield to lash in a couple of goals and bring Celtic to their knees again. The

Celtic faithful looked down in anguish, praying for a touch of green-and-white greatness to turn the game back in their favour, and the hour supplied the man; the wee man at inside right. Up the field bounced Bobby like a veritable jack-in-the-box. He sensed that the whole Clyde defence was about to descend on him and here the Collins timing was only equalled by the Collins genius. From 30 yards, and while still on the run, he unleashed the mother and father of all 'banana' drives. Like an arrow the ball left his foot. A second later the ball was high in the side of the net. What a goal! What a perfect time to score it! What a reviver and inspiration to his colleagues! Celtic had more dig, and they had Collins, and that's why they are now high and dry in the League Cup final.'

Following this success, Bobby lined up for a match that has gone into club folklore. Celtic's 7-1 thrashing of Rangers in the 1957 Scottish League Cup final is still the biggest margin of victory ever recorded in Scotland or England in a League Cup final forty-seven years on. By far the most humiliating defeat in Rangers' history, Bobby recalled a match dubbed 'Seven Past Niven' in the *Weekly News*.

Celtic *v.* Rangers, Scottish League Cup final

Celtic: Beattie, Donnelly, Fallon, Fernie, Evans, Peacock, Tully, Collins, McPhail, Wilson, Mochan
Rangers: Niven, Shearer, Caldow, McColl, Valentine, Davis, Scott, Simpson, Murray, Baird, Hubbard

It was a dream of a game for us, but it must have been a nightmare for Johnny Valentine. Rangers had signed the big centre half from Queen's Park at the start of the season but he simply hadn't clicked. On this day at Hampden, I don't know if Valentine had no faith in George Niven or Niven had no faith in Valentine, but ultimately they had no faith in themselves, something you can sense very quickly on a football field, and inevitably the game became a rout.

Valentine was covering Billy McPhail and McColl and Davis were covering Valentine, which left three of our men with the freedom of Hampden. Rangers' defenders were standing on their heels when Sammy Wilson slammed home goal number one in 22 minutes. They were standing on their heads when Neilly Mochan rammed in number two just before half-time. They say Rangers' mistakes in the first half were because of too much sun in their eyes, but the truth is there had been too much Celtic in their eyes!

By the time we came out for the second half we had sensed that 'something' was on. We could scarcely put a foot wrong. The ball sped from toe to toe. Donnelly to Fernie, Fernie to Tully, Tully to me, over to Mochan and so on. Just to vary things, the ball often stopped at Willie Fernie. Willie kept the entertainment going. And every now and then we slotted in another goal.

Billy McPhail took a joint gift from Niven and Valentine to make it three. A good flying header by Billy Simpson reduced our lead, but somehow it didn't seem to matter. We just carried on, playing our football and we scored another four.

Seven past Niven!

Twice I hit the bar with 30-yard free kicks. McPhail nodded in to make it 4-1. Neilly Mochan duffed a kick, yet still saw his shot enter the net. Billy McPhail stepped in to complete his hat-trick, then with the last kick of the game, Willie Fernie got his own souvenir of the occasion. Shearer fouled McPhail...Penalty! Fernie took the kick. The ball landed low in the net. The time-up whistle blew.

It's always seemed to me the whole game was summed up in that final, dramatic moment. Summed up by Willie Fernie getting all the congrats form the entire Celts team. Summed up by the ball finding its final resting place in Rangers' net, where it had nestled so often in this fantastic game.

It was the biggest-ever victory to be chalked up in a competitive Old Firm game and as a special favour, the Celtic players were allowed to keep their jerseys as a souvenir of the great day.

Charlie Tully captured the triumph with a calypso: 'Oh Hampden in the sun, Celtic seven Rangers one. Charlie Tully did a dance, and had the Rangers in a trance.' To this day it's a game that brings a wry smile to Bobby!

Looking back the result was just sensational and supporters will never forget the 7-1 triumph against Rangers because we were not expected to win, but we thumped them that day.

It was just one of those games when everything went right for us. That said we played some great football and thoroughly deserved our win in the end. It's great to be remembered as being part of this game, and one I'm proud to be associated with.

Bobby waits to pounce as Niven claims the ball during the cup final.

Cup winners! *From left to right, back row:* Goldie, Fallon, Beattie, McPhail, Fernie, Evans. *Front row:* Johnstone (trainer), Tully, Collins, Peacock, Wilson, Mochan, McGrory (manager). Displaying the Scottish League Cup, only Donnelly is missing from the team that destroyed Rangers.

SIX

WORLD CUP WOE
1957-1958

On the representative scene Bobby scored a hat-trick for the Scottish League in a 5-1 win against the League of Ireland in Dublin. A fine win, yet the media slated Scotland. '5 Goals - But What A Flop!' screamed the *Daily Record*. 'This was an easy win for Scotland but certainly not an impressive one. Up front there was plenty cause for censure. Except for a short period midway through the second half, our attack failed to click. Collins, despite a hat-trick and Kelly lacked guile and nearly all the game occupied the role of opportunists... On 11 minutes Bauld cut out to the left and moved forward past the right-back. The goalkeeper ran out and Bauld slipped the ball to Collins who smashed it into the empty goal. After 57 minutes Collins, in an all-in assault, hit the ball past Kelly with the Irish defence in a mix-up. Shortly after, Brown cleared the ball to McColl, who cracked it downfield. It was pounced on by Collins who, against a spreadeagled defence taken by surprise, calmly tapped the ball into net.'

It was amazing some of the headlines that appeared at times. What more could we do than win convincingly? Some reports were farcical.

After a warm-up clash against Northern Ireland, in October 1957, Scotland faced Switzerland to claim a place in the World Cup finals. The Scots duly won 3-2. After the game a debate raged surrounding the validity of Scotland's third goal by right-winger Alex Scott. Robert Russell of the *Scottish Daily Express* interviewed personalities involved:

Reg Leafe (referee): 'Scott certainly looked offside to me, but before the match I had instructed the linesmen that if there was no infringement they were to run back towards midfield. That's what happened so I allowed the goal to stand. The Swiss players wanted me to consult the linesman, but that would have been a sign of weakness. He had made his decision, and was in the best position to do so. I was not in a position to question it.'

G. Hartley (linesman): 'Scott was onside when Collins played the ball. That is the vital thing. What Scott's position was when he got the ball is beside the point. Scott's speed took him on to the ball, and deceived the spectators and the Swiss defenders.'

Alex Scott: 'I was watching the ball the whole time, and had no idea of the position of the defenders. I don't know whether I was offside or not. I just played to the whistle.'

Eric Caldow and Bobby grab a lift from a friendly Irish cabby.

The media wrote off Scotland's chances in Sweden:

Tommy Muirhead in the *Scottish Daily Express*: 'World Cup…We don't have a 1000-1 chance on this form. There was no harmony and understanding. Everyone seemed to be obsessed by the necessity to win and qualify for the World Cup. In individual skill, teamwork and accuracy the Swiss were miles ahead of the Scots.'

Cyril Horne in the *Glasgow Herald*: 'The final stages of the tournament are seven months off; in the interval Scotland's selectors and footballers have a tremendous task. For on the evidence of yesterday the visit to Sweden is necessary and worthwhile only to assimilate further knowledge of how to play football. Yesterday's Scottish team would have been massacred by Hungary of a year or two ago or by several other countries of world football renown.'

Despite the negative media, for Bobby Collins, the group stages had been a personal success. Playing in all four games, he had been influential in them all and scored a vital goal in the victory in Basle.

Spain's demise was a surprise to many because they boasted the greatest club side in European football in Real Madrid and had been expected to breeze past their opponents. However they failed and that was in no small part due to our never-say-die spirit. When I saw some of the reports the following day, I was amazed. Anyone would have thought we had lost. Okay, we weren't sensational and had performed better in other games, but we had just qualified for the World Cup finals, surely the result was everything? It was for me, winning is everything in football. Nobody remembers a loser.

During the build up to the World Cup finals, selectors announced that they would select a full squad of twenty-two, not a team and two reserves as in 1954. The squad would also be paid £3,250 for their efforts against Poland and the initial three World Cup qualifying games. The first team would collect £50 per game, totalling £2,200; the 11 reserves picking up £30 per game, totalling £1,320. Should the side make it further the bonus rate would continue per round all the way to the final.

Scotland XI *v.* Northern Ireland, October 1957. *From left to right, back row:* McColl, Evans, Younger, Parker, Caldow. *Front row:* Leggat, Collins, Mudie, Docherty, Baird, Ring.

Prior to the World Cup finals, Bobby missed just one game, an utterly forgettable 4-0 defeat at the hands of England. The gloom was soon lifted however, following a confidence boosting 1-1 draw against Hungary.

Cyril Horne noted in the *Glasgow Herald*: 'For well over an hour Scotland were far the superior side, cheered time and again by many of those who had disparaged the efforts of their predecessors.'

Waverley's viewpoint in the *Daily Record* was: 'Has a new era dawned for Scottish football? Have we found at long last the way back to the days of glory? I cannot bring myself to fault one single Scot.'

Jimmy Stevenson of the *Daily Mirror* felt that: 'Rain-soaked but hearty, the fans loved this Scotland. Craft and class did it and a Haggis skin full of guts.'

Skipper Tommy Younger told John Mackenzie of the *Scottish Daily Herald*: 'Give the Hungarians a wee bit of credit. They cottoned on to the game we were trying to play and took measures to counter it. It meant that our boys had to pull out a bit extra to cope with them. I think they succeeded. The wingers kept nipping back to collect the ball from the wing halves and they followed back to tackle when necessary. Bobby Collins had a roving commission behind the forward line. On the whole it worked well.'

Hungarian coach Carlos Sos added: 'The conditions favoured Scotland. I refuse to judge my team under such conditions. If you are wise, you will not judge the Scottish team either. They will find the grounds in very different shape in Sweden.'

The final warm up match resulted in a hard-fought 2-1 win in Poland; a match in which Bobby took his tally of goals to 5 with another brace. His first goal hit the goalkeeper, an upright and the 'keeper again before crossing the line. The second was more sublime, a long-range strike from 35 yards that curled into the goal. Bobby Collins said:

I was delighted to get two goals, but I thought we should have had a third when the Polish goalkeeper knocked the ball over the line in the second half. However, we're pretty happy. After all it's great to start with a win. Now for Sweden.

Selectors announced Scotland's twenty-two-man squad for the finals:
Younger (Liverpool), Brown (Dundee), Caldow (Rangers), Hewie (Charlton), Parker (Everton), Haddock (Clyde), Turnbull (Hibernian), Evans (Celtic), Cowie (Dundee), Docherty (Preston), McColl (Rangers), Mackay (Hearts), Leggat (Aberdeen), Murray (Hearts), Mudie (Blackpool), Collins (Celtic), Imlach (Nottingham Forest), Scott (Rangers), Baird (Rangers), Coyle (Clyde), Robertson (Clyde), Fernie (Celtic).

For many observers the sixth World Cup finals was the first true tournament. Apart from Uruguay and Spain no major nation was missing, more importantly, the sixteen competing nations had all pre-qualified; not so in previous tournaments. In 1950 three teams who had qualified chose not to travel to Brazil, and the two previous tournaments had seen FIFA use the Home International tournament as a British qualification group. At last, French legislator Jules Rimet's global dream of a world tournament was a reality. The winners would be the undisputed Champions of world football.

Poles apart... Bobby goes close.

Scotland's previous participation in finals had not been memorable. In 1950 their own bizarre 'internal' rules meant that they would only participate if they won the Home International tournament. They qualified as runners-up but chose not travel to Brazil. They did compete in 1954 but it was a shambles. After losing to Austria 1-0, manager Andy Beattie, the first manager appointed to the post, resigned, citing interference from selectors. Unsurprisingly the dispirited side were trounced 7-0 by Uruguay to seal their fate. The Scottish Football Association needed a manager. They had asked Matt Busby, manager of Manchester United's 'Busby Babes', prior to the clash with Switzerland that sealed their place in Sweden, but his injuries suffered in the Munich air disaster, which cost the lives of many of his star side, including Duncan Edwards, Tommy Taylor and Roger Byrne, meant a rethink.

When the competition finally kicked off, British supporters followed the fortunes of four home nations: England, Scotland, Wales and Northern Ireland.

Scotland XI *v.* Yugoslavia, World Cup: Younger, Caldow, Hewie, Turnbull, Evans, Cowie, Leggat, Murray, Mudie, Collins, Imlach

In their opening fixture, Scotland drew 1-1 with Yugoslavia in Eskilstuna. However, but for a hotly disputed disallowed goal, they would have won. Pundits agreed that

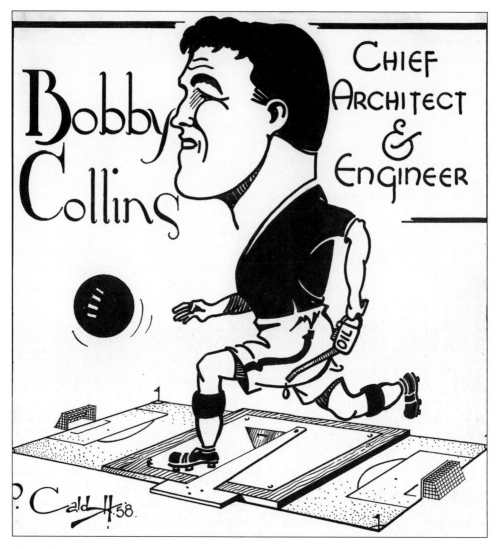

Top man!

Scotland were robbed and performed heroically in the face of appalling Yugoslavian tactics.

Cyril Horne commented in the *Glasgow Herald*: 'Beara, Yugoslavia's goalkeeper master of aerobics and dramatics, rose in condescending fashion for a cross from Imlach, descended on the challenging Mudie, and lost the ball, which crossed his goal line. The few Scots in the crowd of little more than 9,500 and the many Swedish folk, who had long before displayed their support for Scotland, went into delirium of delight. I showed no comparable enthusiasm; indeed I was not surprised when one of the worst referees of all time awarded a free-kick against Mudie while Beara rolled on the ground in histrionic agony. Scotland's footballers and selectors have answered their biased bigoted critics. The quarter-finals gleam brightly ahead.'

Gair Henderson of the *Evening Times* felt similarly: 'They (Yugoslavia) were adept at every aspect of obstruction and destruction. They pushed their bodies between the Scots and the ball at every opportunity, and they were given a free hand by a referee whose tolerance of these tactics and his intolerance of the Scottish tackling had to be seen to be believed.'

Hugh Taylor of the *Evening Citizen* agreed: 'This was Scotland the brave, Scotland the soccer masters. At home the goal that was disallowed would have caused a break-in. Even the 9,500 polite Swedes who watched shook their heads in amazement when it was disallowed. Everything was against them. They were the victims of refereeing decisions which would have been out of place even in a Marx Brothers film, and assaults which would have worried Floyd Patterson.'

Bobby's performance was deservedly acclaimed.

Hugh Taylor felt that 'Wee Bobby Collins, playing his greatest international, came to our rescue. Collins was inspired. He took command of the game. How the hard men from Titoland knew that. They tried to crash him out of the game. First right-

Ready to take on the world.

back Sitjakovic got him when his back was turned and sent him reeling to the ground. Bobby got up, shook his head and shook it again when he saw referee Wyssling wave play-on instead of ordering off the Slav. Next Bobby suddenly stopped short and put his hand to his mouth after Sekularac had elbowed him in the face. How I admired Collins, criticised so often for his impetuosity, for his restraint in this match. He paused only to put in more firmly two loosened teeth, and played even more brilliantly.'

Bobby also earned praise from Cyril Horne: 'Collins repeatedly frustrated his opponent with his inimitable combination of nippiness and almost incredible strength for one so tiny as footballers go, and with the reaction of a boxer tormented by a more nimble adversary the Yugoslavs (especially Sekularic) indulged in multifarious activities not covered by Queensbury rules. To his everlasting credit he restrained himself and continued until the end, by which time he was pardonably showing slight signs of exhaustion after his superlative effort.'

The result saw Scotland's odds shrink from 33-1 to 12-1. In fact one leading bookmaker in Glasgow reduced the odds to 10-1. Their next challenge would be challenging though as they faced Paraguay, defeated 7-3 by France in their opening group match. The South Americans could dazzle but generally had a reputation for being hot-headed and cynical.

Scotland XI *v.* Paraguay, World Cup: Younger, Parker, Caldow, Turnbull, Evans, Cowie, Leggat, Collins, Mudie, Robertson, Fernie

A combination of puzzling decisions by the Italian referee and cynical defending resulted in a 3-2 defeat. At 3-1 behind, Bobby scored 14 minutes from time, but Scotland were unable to grab a share of the spoils.

Alec Young of the *Scottish Daily Mail* felt: 'It was disappointing, after a brilliant display against one of the favourites for the Cup that they should slump so badly against Paraguay.'

Scotland's fate now depended on how they fared against France at the Eyravallen Stadium.

Scotland XI *v.* France, World Cup: Brown, Caldow, Hewie, Turnbull, Evans, Mackay, Collins, Murray, Mudie, Baird, Imlach

Scotland battled manly but went out of the competition following a 2-1 defeat. While they were never really in the game, but for a missed penalty by John Hewie when the French were leading 1-0, they just might have caused a surprise.

Tommy Muirhead's thoughts in the *Scottish Daily Express* were: 'I have nothing but praise and admiration for our players. The changes made by the selectors were more than justified. Bill Brown, in his very first international, played magnificently, and repeatedly came to our rescue. Evans was a grand general and an inspiring captain. Davie Mackay was not excelled by any other wing half. The attack unfortunately sparked on only three cylinders...Collins, Murray and Baird. These three ran themselves into

Final preparations before the crunch match with Paraguay.

the ground. For us the match was one of what might have been. Yes it was a great match and a gallant failure. And the Scots party, which arrives home at Prestwick on Tuesday, may be sad, but for tonight at least, there is little call for them to be ashamed.'

Cyril Horne was philosophical in the *Glasgow Herald*: 'We leave Sweden on Tuesday sadder but wiser men. The main lesson that must surely have been learned is that for all the hard work behind the scenes in the preparation for such a venture as this, the effort is profitless if the fundamental art of scoring goals is lost.'

Regarding the fate of the other home nations, England went out in a group play-off against Russia. Northern Ireland won a thrilling play-off against Czechoslovakia before losing in the quarter-finals to France but pride of place went to Wales who lost to eventual Champions Brazil in the quarter-finals, their hero of the competition being John Charles, who enhanced his growing reputation.

When the dust had settled, observers were critical about tactical errors in playing ball players against cynical opposition like Paraguay, and the decision to sanction the twenty-two-man squad embarking on a six-hour trip to watch Sweden take on Hungary twenty-four hours before another six-hour trip for the game against Paraguay. John Camkin in his book *World Cup 1958* did, however, concede that the margin of Scotland's defeats was small and he had words of encouragement for two players: 'Clearly the land of the thistle possessed footballers of class, men like Bobby Collins and John Hewie, who could hold heads high in any company.'

When I look back at the World Cup in 1958, we could be proud of our efforts. Okay we failed to reach the quarter-finals, but that was due to the opening game when we

So close… Bobby and Willie Fernie almost grab an equalizer against Paraguay.

were extremely unlucky. The refereeing was questionable to say the least, as it was against Paraguay when we lost. The French were a class act and possessed the top striker of the tournament in their side, Juste Fontaine. Not every footballer gets the opportunity to play in the World Cup. I had and I managed to grab a goal.

SEVEN

MERSEY BEAT
1958-1959

When Bobby returned to training after the World Cup he quickly realised that his career was at a crossroads, even though during an eventful decade with Celtic he'd won every domestic honour and been capped numerous times by his country and Scottish League. Bobby played in the opening two League games, scoring a goal in a 2-0 win against Rangers. It would be his final Old Firm match. In the League Cup, scoring 7 goals in 6 games, his strike in a 2-0 quarter-final first-leg win over Cowdenbeath would be his last for the club. The following day, reports headlined that Bobby Collins was to leave Celtic.

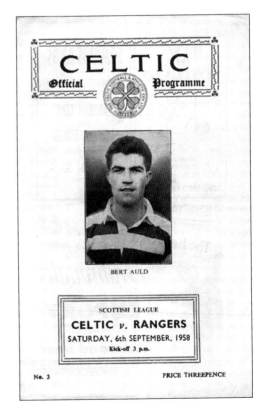

Last Old Firm clash.

Jimmy Carabine wrote of Bobby's last appearance for Celtic in the *Scottish Daily Express*: 'The man who kept them (Celtic) on top for most of the time was Bobby Collins, playing what was probably his last game before a home crowd. The wee fellow was in grand form, sending inch-perfect passes all over the field and always up for a shot at goal. Collins opened the scoring. He took a pass from Smith, rounded Lindsay and beat 'keeper Dorman off the upright… After 67 minutes, Celtic were rewarded for their pressure when Auld headed a brilliant second goal from a Collins cross.'

Celtic manager Jimmy McGrory announced in the paper: 'Bobby Collins' request for a transfer was discussed at a board meeting before the game. The directors reluctantly decided to consider offers for his transfer.'

Behind the scenes things weren't ideal. Jock Stein, Billy McPhail and Sean Fallon had retired and Willie Fernie and Charlie Tully would soon depart. The Parkhead team I

Bobby signs on the dotted line for Everton. Watching is Everton director Jack Sharp and Celtic boss Jimmy McGrory.

was an integral part of was breaking up; we'd had our swansong in the League Cup final and I felt that I needed to find a new challenge. I'd been fortunate to play for such a great club because not everyone gets such an opportunity.

The news meant that it would not be long before potential clubs enquired. Bobby quickly heard about an opportunity while playing golf when a message from manager Jimmy McGrory arrived that Everton had offered £23,500.

At first, part of me wondered if there would be any bad feelings after my move broke down a decade earlier, but those reservations disappeared when I discussed terms with their manager Ian Buchan, who had bizarrely taught my brother Archie PT at John Stirling Maxwell School in Glasgow.

Time has not diminished Bobby's popularity with Celtic followers. Lifelong friend Tommy McGrotty recalls: 'Celtic supporters just loved his skill, power and commitment and still talk about him today. One incident summed up Bobby for me. Celtic was playing Rangers in a really tight match and Bobby went into a 50-50 ball with big George Young. George was slightly off balance and ended up on the running track. You could see by the look on his face that he was not pleased, but that was Bobby; total commitment and his efforts will never be forgotten by Celtic fans.'

Everton were a club with an eye on the future. Already possessing floodlights, they became the first British club to install undersoil heating at the end of the 1957/58 campaign. At a cost of £16,000 it was seen as visionary and many clubs would soon follow suit. Sadly the team were not as successful.

Bobby's arrival on 12 September 1958 coincided with the club being in a terrible run of form, having lost their opening six League games of the campaign, including a 6-1 defeat at home to Arsenal. The defeat resulted in chairman Dick Searle openly criticising the team and question the manager's coaching philosophy. Twenty-four hours later Everton had their first victory of the season and Bobby wrapped up a 3-1 victory at Manchester City with a goal. Local papers were ecstatic with the new signing.

In a report titled *Bobby-Dazzler*, the reporter observed: 'The jersey may be unfamiliar, but there's no mistaking the man inside. Yes, it's bouncing Collins helping his new side Everton to their first points of the season. It was a great start for Bobby, and Everton. He was the most accomplished forward afield and scored a golden goal in his side's 3-1 win. But this was not the Collins brand of soccer that set Celtic Park alight. Not once did he go through on his own. Only once, goal excepted, did he trouble Trautmann. 'Kid Dynamite' had left his explosives at home. Instead, he adopted the role of ammunition supplier, a job he carried out admiringly. The Collins viewpoint, apparently, was that in his first game, at any rate, it was much better to play safe. Not to chance the arm with a hit-or-miss, block-busting performance. Result… pinpointed passes that seldom travelled more than 15 yards, and which always topped an erratic City defence on a blind spot. Not until the second half, however, did his teammates take a leaf out of the Collins curriculum. First half they had hurried

Goodison man!

and scurried, with no obvious plan, leaving Collins somewhat flummoxed by it all and a little breathless. Now they slowed the tempo and banged in three goals to wipe out City's interval lead.'

Speaking after the game, Bobby said:

I enjoyed my first game as an Everton player and I thought the team played very well. English football is certainly faster than the Scottish game but I will soon adjust myself. It didn't take long to realise why Everton were in such trouble. I'd been told to stay in attack, but starved of the ball, I foraged in my usual style and managed to grab our opening goal. The manager didn't complain, I think he was relieved that I'd used my initiative.

The result sparked a mini-revival, with Everton winning three of their next four encounters, but it was too late to save Buchan's job as Johnny Carey agreed to become the new manager, though not till the end of October. By then the team would suffer an horrendous 10-4 defeat at Tottenham. Everton were ripped to shreds as Bill Nicholson watched his new charges having taken over as manager at White Hart Lane on the morning of the match. Jimmy Harris was the only Blue to come out

Welcoming the new boss, Johnny Carey.

unscathed having grabbed a hat-trick along with Bobby Collins, who scored the other consolation goal.

Following a 3-2 win over Manchester United, Carey, who had enjoyed a distinguished playing career, representing Eire and captaining the Rest of Europe against Great Britain in a clash dubbed the 'Match of the Century' at Hampden Park shortly after the Second World War, arrived.

Ian Buchan knew the game but he was too much of a theorist, having never played the game at the top level. Johnny on the other hand had a wealth of experience and

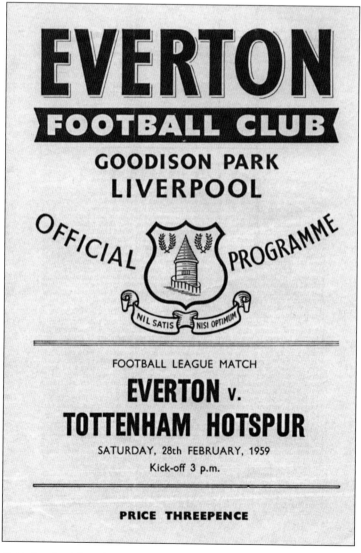

EVERTON

FOOTBALL CLUB

GOODISON PARK
LIVERPOOL

OFFICIAL PROGRAMME

NIL SATIS NISI OPTIMUM

FOOTBALL LEAGUE MATCH

EVERTON v.
TOTTENHAM HOTSPUR

SATURDAY, 28th FEBRUARY, 1959
Kick-off 3 p.m.

PRICE THREEPENCE

Bobby's strike defeats the Spurs.

understood players more as he had been successful in his own playing career. A great tactician, he gave you a job and it was down to the player to make it work.

Results slowly improved with the team gaining 4 wins and 3 draws from their next 10 League fixtures. The run included a welcome 'double' against title hopefuls Bolton Wanderers over Christmas to ease the Blues' relegation fears. Bobby had played throughout this period and had settled into the pattern of play.

Following the 3-0 win at Bolton, reporters were quick to praise Bobby who made two goals and stood out from the crowd. Jim Beecroft felt: 'It was a mud lark for wee Bobby Collins. He bamboozled Bolton's defenders with a dazzling exhibition. Bobby's ball play and distribution were a sheer delight and his energy, on a day demanding unusual stamina and fitness, was fabulous.' Harry Peterson was similarly enthusiastic: 'What a player…what a match-winner! Bobby Collins, the wee Scot with the twinkling feet and impish grin, whose brilliant ball play in the Burnden Park mud gave Bolton's championship hopes an unexpected jolt. Bolton had no answer to the Collins magic. He teased and tormented the Wanderers' defence with inch-perfect passes and immaculate ball control. And when he was not setting the Everton attack in motion, he was in defence helping to break up Bolton attacks. Yes, Collins was brilliant.'

The New Year began with a 4-0 drubbing at Newcastle, one of 6 defeats in a worrying 10-game spell, which brought just 3 wins, one which Bobby inspired with the opening goal in a 2-1 against Tottenham. However, safety was eventually achieved following a three-match winning run during Easter and a 3-2 win at Portsmouth in their penultimate away game of the season. In the FA Cup hopes rose as Everton overcame Blackpool and Charlton Athletic before crashing out to Aston Villa 4-1 at Goodison Park. Bobby scored 3 goals in the clashes against Charlton, but sadly there would be no Wembley trip.

Since making his debut, Bobby had missed only four League and cup matches and had become a firm favourite with supporters. 'The Mighty Atom', as fans dubbed him, had also played against future club Leeds United for the first time. He missed his side's 3-2 win at Goodison but played in a 1-0 defeat at Elland Road. In the Leeds side were Jack Charlton and former England international Don Revie, who made his name as a deep-lying centre forward with Manchester City. Both would become major influences in Bobby's career. The Yorkshire team finished just one place higher than Everton.

On the international scene, Matt Busby felt fit enough to lead his country. With Dave Mackay announced as the new captain of the national team, Scotland began a new dawn with an air of confidence. Four new caps came in for the first match since the World Cup finals against Wales, including Huddersfield Town striker Denis Law. In a superb display the Scots won with ease and Bobby scored a sensational goal. John Blair was euphoric in *The People*:

'Scotland are on the way back! In the fiery white-heat of Cardiff's Ninian Park, and before a 60,000 jam-packed crowd, the blue-shirted Scots teased and tamed a willing but disappointing Wales team into a 3-0 defeat. At long last Scotland have found a forward line and particularly two inside-men who can hold the ball in something like the manner we used to call traditional style. It was the youngest player, Denis Law, and

Matt Busby puts his point across to his new charges (© *The Scottish Daily Record*).

Scotland's XI *v.* Wales, 1959 (© *The Scottish Daily Record*).

Bobby cracks in a fine effort in Scotland's 3-0 win against the Welsh.

the smallest player, Bobby Collins, who laid the foundations of this Scottish victory which warmed the hearts of the thousands of tartan-tammied Scots who swarmed into Cardiff. You can praise Matt Busby for his influence, his advice and pre-match plans, but for my money it was the guile, guts and graft of Collins and Law which made our victory complete.'

Gair Henderson of the *Evening Times* gave most of the credit to Bobby: 'Collins was our number one forward, roaming here, there and everywhere on the field and finding his man with the long pass every time. Eleven minutes from time Collins scored the best goal of his international career. From his foot the ball flew 20 yards into the top of the net after magnificent play by Grant and Docherty.'

Sadly, after the euphoria, Scotland drew 2-2 against Northern Ireland and prior to the clash with England, Busby stepped down as he was not fit enough to combine his duties with Manchester United. Andy Beattie stepped back into the fray, but for the third time Bobby ended on the losing side against England, a match settled by a goal from Bobby Charlton. The match was also memorable as Billy Wright won his 100th cap for England

During the post-season tour Scotland roared back. With the likes of Denis Law, Ian St John and John White now in the team, Scotland were an exciting team to watch, and

FOOTBALL ASSOCIATION INTERNATIONAL

ENGLAND
v
SCOTLAND

SATURDAY, APRIL 11th, 1959   KICK-OFF 3 pm

EMPIRE STADIUM
WEMBLEY

OFFICIAL PROGRAMME   **ONE SHILLING**

Above: Wembley woe.

Opposite: Final preparations for the England clash.

Dutch courage.

following an impressive 3-2 victory at Hampden against West Germany, Bobby scored the opening goal in a fine 2-1 win over Holland. The strike against the Dutch would prove to be his seventh and last for his country. Bobby faced Portugal a few days later, a match the Scots lost to a solitary goal, but by the start of the new season he was out of the frame for selection. At the time many pundits believed his international days were over. Bobby would prove them wrong.

EIGHT

BATTLING BLUES
1959-1961

The new manager may have stabilized the club but the 1959/60 campaign began in a similar manner to the previous season as Everton failed to win a game until their seventh match. By the end of October, supporters were disgruntled, especially after Gwladys Street favourite Dave Hickson joined Liverpool. The striker's departure saw Bobby Collins become club captain and the players responded with a 6-1 win at home to Leicester City; the new skipper grabbing his third goal of the League campaign. However, fans voiced their frustrations a week later when Hickson scored twice on his Liverpool debut and Everton crashed 8-2 at Newcastle United. Undaunted, the players bounced back with a 4-0 win against Birmingham, but inconsistency kept them in the lower reaches of the table despite a number of inspiring performances which included irresistible displays against Nottingham Forest and Chelsea who were both thumped 6-1. The results kept Everton above the relegation zone.

Following the win against Forest, Albert Geldard of the *Sunday Post* wrote: 'At last a day of joy for Everton. After failing to score in their last four matches, their goal-shy attack warmed the hearts of their supporters by scoring six times. Collins again was the schemer of almost every Everton attack.' As for the win over Chelsea, who included the mercurial Jimmy Greaves in their line-up, Derek Wallis observed in the *Daily Mirror*: 'Bobby Collins has made nonsense of all transfer fees. You couldn't buy Johnny Haynes for that, Jimmy McIlory or Albert Quixall. I cannot remember a greater display of all the inside forward's subtle skills since the war than the torture of Chelsea by Collins.'

A 6-2 defeat at West Brom raised doubts again, but an unbeaten six-match run, which included wins against Tottenham, Blackpool and Leeds United, edged Everton away from the relegation zone. The win over title-chasing Tottenham Hotspur, who eventually finished third, 2 points adrift of Champions Burnley, had been particularly impressive and belied their lowly status. A goal down to the Londoners at the interval, a Jimmy Harris header and a Bobby Collins drive earned a hard-fought victory. Don Evans commented: 'Collins was weaving the patterns, from which the match was won. For Spurs it was a sad day, one which could cost them the title. Not that they were without class, indeed, they overflowed with it. For copybook soccer many of their moves would have taken the headmaster's prize. But when it is points you are after, forward punch is often a greater asset. Spurs seldom looked like providing it. Everton often did. The scoreline was as simple as that.'

Everton 1959/60. *From left to right, back row:* Jones, Rea, Parker, Dunlop, Bramwell, Meagan, Tansey, Watson (trainer). *Front row:* Sanders, J. Harris, Thomas, Hickson, Collins, O'Hara, B. Harris.

The clash at Goodison over Easter against mid-table Blackpool was pivotal in Everton's survival. Terence Elliot, writing in the *Daily Express* was complimentary: 'The Goodison crowd can now let out a great sigh of relegation relief. Even Stan Matthews must take a back seat. He could not shake Blackpool into their old magic ways. Everton's second goal was brilliant. Bobby Collins, he shares Man of the Match honours with centre half Brian Labone, was bang on the spot when Jimmy Harris battled his way past left-back Martin to crash the ball low across the face of the goal. If Collins had stopped the ball it would have been pounced on by the Blackpool defence. He didn't. He glided a first time shot into the far corner of the net.'

Horace Yates wrote in the *Liverpool Daily Post*: 'Although the ageless magician Matthews was in the Blackpool ranks, still producing the touches which gave the crowd opportunity to applaud his acknowledged genius, he had to take second place to the more youthful, more mobile Everton wonder, Bobby Collins. While Matthews has learned in these advanced days not to overdo individual effort, Collins thrived on hard labour and set up movement after movement by dispossessing an opponent. The scoring of the fourth goal in 81 minutes was a typical example of his enterprise. Taking the ball from Perry in a tackle inside his own half, he went on to beat Martin with ridiculous ease. So completely left was the Blackpool full-back that he did not even bother to chase. Collins shot the ball forward immaculately for Lill, whose cross passed invitingly in front of the goal for Jimmy Harris to score at his leisure. Had we not seen so much of the Collins brilliance, his display would have looked even better, but we have now reached the stage where our expectations are so high that on occasions when they are not fulfilled disappointment is possibly unduly great. This game must rank as one of the best Collins has ever served up.'

The campaign had gone well for Bobby Collins, despite the team's inconsistency, especially away from home where they failed to win a League game and in the FA Cup when they went out in the third round following a demoralising 3-0 defeat at lowly Bradford City. Top scorer with 14 goals, Bobby's 6 strikes in 7 matches during the League run-in proved essential in the side's ultimate survival.

Respected throughout the League, Bobby Collins' adaptation to English football was complete. England and Blackburn Rovers skipper Ronnie Clayton rated Everton's skipper one of the most difficult players he had faced. In an article in *The Pink*, Clayton noted, 'One inside left whom I have seen much too often for my liking is former Celtic player Bobby Collins of Everton. Every player has a bogeyman, Bobby Collins has always

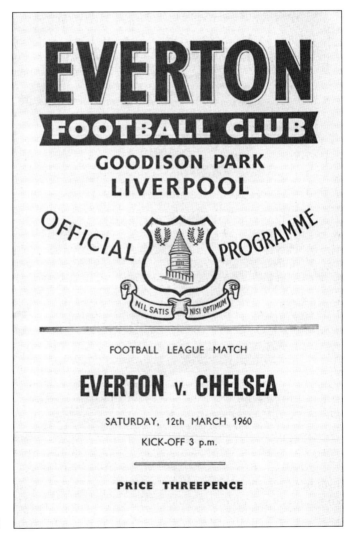

Six of the best!

been mine. Undoubtedly he has been the most difficult opponent I have ever played against, and I was always glad and still am if I'm on the winning side after a game against the effervescent Robert, who runs on the field and never stops running until it's finished.'

Things had to change if Everton were to become a force again. Fortunately, behind the scenes Everton had the financial backing of director John Moores, founder of the Littlewoods empire. With his help, players began to arrive at the club, the best signings proving to be Roy Vernon and Jimmy Gabriel. During the close-season, Moores was elected club chairman and made his intentions clear at the club's annual general meeting. He said: 'Everton must have the best players, the best coaches, the best manager and the best directors. If any of them fail, they must go.'

With the squad getting stronger, Everton's star striker Roy Vernon, who joined in February 1960, talked about the influence of Bobby Collins at Goodison Park in a local paper: 'I have never played with a more talented, complete inside forward, a greater bundle of tricks and a more regular powerhouse than this diminutive Scot. Nor have I ever played against an inside forward of any other club who has left me with a feeling that here is somebody even better than Collins. He is a buy in a lifetime. Where he gets his boundless energy from I don't pretend to know. He never complains at hard work, rather does he thrive on it. It is a gift that some players have, which others cannot acquire if they play for years, the ability to take the game by the scruff of the neck and play it at the tempo required. There are times when games seem to go mad with players scurrying around at break-neck speed, making their work much more difficult and the margin for error ever so much more greater. How useful it is as a time like this to have a man, who almost imperceptibly applies the brake and becomes the dictator.

What is Collins like off the field? Just the same as he is on it. A cheerful, cheeky little chappie, always ready for a joke and a leg pull, good company at any time and with the sort of temperament that is a boon to any club. From the game's point of view the pity is that there are so few Bobby Collins's, but imagine what a headache we would have if we had players like him in opposition every week! I rate Collins one of the personalities of our time, and that is not merely because I happen to play alongside him, but the privilege of doing so helps me to see his cleverness at close quarters. Nobody can tell me that money does not matter to any player, but while there are some who play the game because it is a livelihood, Collins is one who makes playing a pleasure. He really enjoys his football.'

During the close season, Bobby travelled to South Africa to play a number of games for Southern Suburbs. His first game was played in Port Elizabeth. Local papers commented: 'Scottish soccer international Bobby Collins, who played his first game in South Africa here today was the star of Southern Suburbs 2-1 win over Eastern Province. A goal ahead, halfway through the second half the dynamic Collins slammed in a terrific goal for his side's second. Province pulled a goal back, and in their efforts to get the equalizer play was a bit robust for some 10 minutes. Nevertheless the game was always fast and entertaining, Collins excelling before a crowd of just on 1,500.'

Suburbs were one of the worst sides in the league, but his brief time with them was sufficient to help his side create history when they shattered the proud record of

Durban teams in the National Football League of never having been beaten by a Transvaal team in Durban.

I scored twice in this match and made our other goal. The lads were ecstatic.

While in South Africa, Bobby played for a Stanley Matthews XI, while helping out Matthews with coaching clinics. The local press was out in force for a clash against a Natal XI. 'Stanley Matthews, Bobby Collins and nine Maritzburg soccer players humbled a Natal XI to the tune of five clear goals before a crowd of more than 4,000 in Maritzburg. As a match it was virtually over long before half-time. The very genius of Matthews, coupled with the astute service of the diminutive Collins, gave Maritzburg a soccer treat never before seen in the capital.

Four goals ahead, Collins having smashed in the third, the second half was an exhibition of delightful ball manipulation and positioning mainly by Matthews and Collins.'

It was a wonderful experience, especially getting together with Stan again. His popularity was just incredible. The support he received in South Africa was amazing. Everyone knew him.

Back home, Bobby prepared for the new season. Everton now appeared a force to be reckoned with. Bobby got the 1960/61 campaign off to a flying start at Goodison Park with a brace against Manchester United in a 4-0 win and a strike against Leicester City, the game finishing 3-1. He also scored in a 4-1 victory at Blackpool to end his side's twenty-five-match run without an away win in the League. Reporter Michael Charters observed: 'This was a solid, convincing victory in which every man in the team played well and some very well indeed. Some of their football was brilliant in design and execution, often impudent in its smooth progression as the ball swept from man to man to bewilder and bamboozle a Blackpool side which was made to look second-rate when they are far from that rating. The burden of this away hoodoo was telling on them but having broken the jinx in the most impressive way, their confidence in their ability to make a real show this season will have increased immeasurably. Collins was typical Collins…always working, always doing something useful, with his passes perfectly placed and schemed to the inch to do the most damage to the opposing defence.'

Charters was correct in his viewpoint. The victory was the start of 5 consecutive wins as Everton moved into third place after 10 matches. The Blues were now being talked of as contenders. More players arrived in the shape of Billy Bingham and Hearts duo Alex Young and George Thomson. Everton's impressive form continued with only 2 defeats in 12 matches. Bobby chipped in with 6 goals including strikes against Chelsea, Manchester City and his first Everton hat-trick in a 5-0 thumping against Newcastle United.

Reporters eulogised. Frank McGhee (*v.* Manchester City in the *Daily Mirror*): 'Manchester City has a world-class inside forward in Denis Law. Everton have two just as great in Roy Vernon and Bobby Collins. Everything City had Everton had, plus a little bit more. Collins was just about the best attacker on the field and very nearly the best defender too.'

Jack Wood (*v.* Manchester City in the *Daily Mail*): 'The impudent genius of a dumpy, fresh-faced Scot called Bobby Collins dominated this game and guided superb Everton to a victory which, but for the greatness of Bert Trautmann, might have been doubly impressive in the scoreline. Inevitably the crowd made their way home comparing Collins with his rival for a Scotland place Denis Law, and without doubt the Everton man came out a clear points winner. Everton are now one of the most attractive and effective sides in the country. They have the impish genius of Collins, the artistry and shooting power of Vernon and a half-back line which for class must rate with the Spurs middle trio.'

Reporter John Leslie (*v.* Newcastle United): 'In their programme Everton warned spectators about pickpockets. They might have added a paragraph for Newcastle's benefit about ace goal-stealer Bobby Collins. Newcastle's defence was shaken into a shambles by pop-up anywhere Bobby. He struck first in the 34th minute when he crashed home a rebound from the crossbar. In the 50th minute, a shot from his right foot slid through Harvey's hands. Three minutes later he peppered Newcastle's goalkeeper again to steer a crisp volley into an empty net. Newcastle were no match for that sort of KO soccer. Everton were great, terrific and wonderful. Vernon's graceful craft was supported by Collins lust for goals and the thrusting speed of both wingers. It was a team win for Everton. There was not a weak link in a side with poise, craft and string.'

I recall the clash against Chelsea because I grabbed a goal in our 3-3 draw, but it came after I had a penalty disallowed as a player had come into the penalty area. The 'keeper saved my second attempt, but I managed to score from the rebound. It was a case of third time lucky! Sometimes everything you try comes off. The match against Newcastle was one such game and I was delighted to grab a hat-trick. The win though was far more important.

During the build up to Christmas, Birmingham City were beaten 4-2 in a fierce encounter. Alan Williams' comments in the *Daily Express* were: 'Inside-left Collins masterminded this so-efficient Everton machine to a hard-earned and just-about-deserved success. He never stopped working and clipped his passes around with a precision that eventually brought the Birmingham defence, so strong in the first half, to its knees. Collins also filled in capably at wing-half when sturdy Brian Harris was off for a spell just after the interval with a cut knee. His qualities made the vital difference in helping Everton pull round after twice being behind.'

Birmingham wing-half Dick Neal said: 'It was hard enough for the big chaps to whip the ball about in the mud. Collins might have been the smallest in stature but he was certainly the biggest in football achievement.'

The win sent the team in good heart to championship leaders Tottenham Hotspur, beaten just once in 21 games, however a 3-1 defeat meant that the Londoners had recorded a double over the title pretenders (Spurs would go on record a First Division

Everton 1960/61. *From left to right, back row:* Parker, Gabriel, Labone, Dunlop, Bramwell, Jones, Watson (trainer). *Front row:* Meagan, Lill, Collins, J. Harris, Vernon, Ring, B. Harris.

and FA Cup double). The clash coincided with Bobby Collins passing a century of games for Everton. Local papers recorded his impact in a special sports edition prior to the clash with Tottenham: 'He is the greatest thing that has happened at Goodison Park since Dixie Dean. This dynamo of a man, better than a dynamo because he never runs down, arrived here in the Ian Buchan era when Everton's position was pretty desperate and some general was urgently needed to take command of their attack. Arsenal, who also wanted him, missed the boat by a mere half-hour.

'Everton's climb began from the day he arrived, though it was some months before that other architect of their rehabilitation, John Carey, was tempted from Blackburn. Initially, Collins found he was wanted as much in defence as he was in attack. Now, with the side more balanced, he can concentrate on his real mission, getting the side on the offensive and keeping them there.

'Wee Bobby lacks nothing in courage either. He'll tackle the biggest and strongest and still come out, more often than not, with the ball at his feet. Collins makes goals or takes them with equal facility. He, more than anyone, has helped his club to win back thousands of 'lost' spectators by ensuring that they will get 90 minutes of effort and football entertainment.

His signing was something of a gamble, but rarely can one man's presence in a team have had such far-reaching effects. Time was when there was talk of him wanting to go back home. I hope it never comes to that. He has established himself as surely in our hearts as that other Scot, Billy Liddell.'

Despite the loss, pundits expected Everton to push on, but after a Boxing Day win over Burnley, the side inexplicably lost 9 of the next 12 League encounters. They also crashed out of both domestic cup competitions; in the inaugural League Cup to Shrewsbury Town and to Sheffield United at home in the FA Cup. It was a bitter blow.

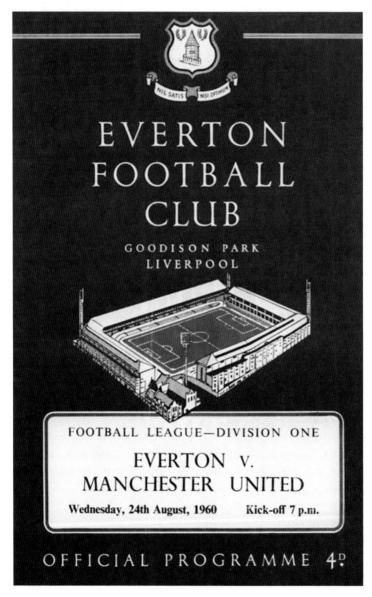

A classy brace
beats Busby's men.

Hat-trick hero.

The end of the season did bring a renaissance with 6 victories in the final 7 matches, but for the manager it was too late. During the team's late purple patch John Moores sacked Carey following a 4-0 victory at Newcastle United. Supporters voiced their disapproval in the next home game when Cardiff were defeated 5-1, a match that saw Bobby grab his second Everton treble, but Moores was determined to move forward. Within two days he introduced ex-Everton centre forward Harry Catterick as the new manager.

Johnny insisted that we enjoyed our football. The only flaw he had was that he wasn't hard enough with the players and some did take liberties. Discipline was not tight enough and this stopped him from becoming a great manager. Top managers need a ruthless streak, as players do, if they want to make at the highest level.

Moores saw Catterick as a bright young manager. He'd guided Sheffield Wednesday to the Second Division title and semi-finals of the FA Cup. He was convinced he would deliver the goods. Ironically Catterick's first game at the helm was against his former charges and Everton duly left Hillsborough with a 2-1 win. A 4-1 win over Arsenal on

AN ARTIST'S IMPRESSION OF TO-DAY'S EVERTON TEAM

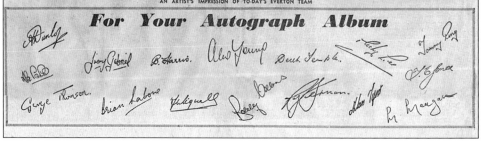

For Your Autograph Album

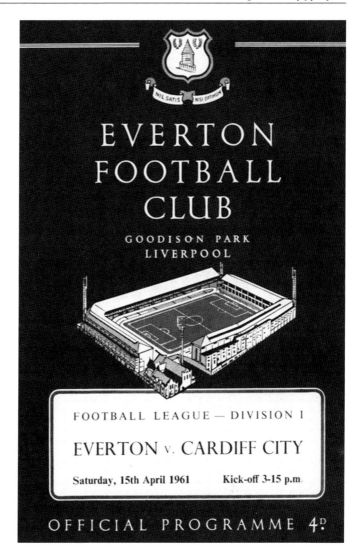

Right: Another treble.

Opposite: Merry Christmas... *Liverpool Echo* and *Evening Gazette,* 1960.

the last day of the season secured fifth place. For Bobby Collins, the season had once again gone well. Missing just two games, he finished second top-scorer behind Vernon in the League and third overall with a total of 18 goals. Frank Wignall ended runner-up, just one behind Vernon's 23 strikes.

Overall it had been a fine season as a lot of progress had been made. With new arrivals and a number of promising youngsters coming through, the immediate future looked promising.

NINE

BLUE TO WHITE
1961-1962

Looking to build on the progress from the previous term, it was something of a surprise when Everton began the new campaign slowly with only 4 victories being gained from their opening 10 League fixtures. Bobby only played two of these games due to an injury sustained at West Brom but his return at Goodison against Arsenal coincided with a run of 6 wins in 7 games. One further defeat before the turn of the year saw Everton sitting comfortably near the top of the table. There had been some impressive home victories; most notably against Arsenal 4-1, Nottingham Forest 6-0 and Wolves 3-0.

Following the clash against the Gunners, Edgar Turner in the *Sunday Pictorial* noted: 'You could tell it was going to be an occasion from the moment Arthur Ellis, stepping out to referee his last match at Goodison, was applauded all the way to the centre spot. It was, but not for Arsenal. With measured tread, they started like slow marching guardsman at the Trooping of the Colour but in next to no time the bullets were whizzing round their ears. Yes, Everton sent a message to Spurs that they had better look out next season. If Everton had rammed home 10, not one of the 40,000 spectators would have been surprised. Collins and co, with full-backs Parker and Thomson, playing with the artistry of forwards, got round after round of applause and thoroughly deserved it.'

Another knock meant Bobby missed a fine 3-0 win over defending champions Tottenham but he was soon back in the side that hammered Manchester United 5-1, a match in which he grabbed his first goal of the season. More goals followed against Aston Villa and Fulham, but the manager was not impressed with his overall form.

After scoring two against Fulham, Catterick told me I was not the player I used to be. I was not happy and told him so. I'd been the best Everton player that day and I'd got a rollicking. I knew that my days were numbered.

There may have been problems internally, but off the field Bobby was in constant demand. In this extract from the *Topical Times* annual, 1961/62, *Muscles Man – In Miniature* provides an amusing insight into Bobby's eating habits and vital statistics to the most minuscule detail:

Double top against Fulham.

'He was the toast of Celtic Park, Glasgow. Now he's top of the poll at Goodison Park, Liverpool. He's Bobby Collins, one of football's great little men. And he does it all – or nearly all – on toast. Bobby's breakfast on match days is toast. He has toast at lunchtime, with maybe an egg. Occasionally he may have a bit of chicken, but no matter what, he still produces as much punch and vitality in 90 minutes of soccer as players who look twice his size.

'Bobby is five feet three and a quarter inch tall. He is a little fussy about that quarter inch. He has never weighed as much as 10 stone, and likes to keep as near 9.7 as possible. When he was transferred to Everton some people wondered if the faster, tougher football in England would be quite his cup of tea. They needn't have worried; Bobby has been as great in England as he was in Scotland.

'He rarely has anything approaching a bad game. Very often his forceful example is a decisive factor in a match. Out on the pitch, in one of the most exacting positions of all, Bobby Collins plays with grit, skill, and enthusiasm. Backing these qualities is an unusually powerful muscle structure. Alex Dowdells, Celtic and Scotland trainer before he joined Leicester City, says that if he were to be blindfolded and given a team (including Bobby Collins) to massage, he could tell which was Bobby by the feel of the leg muscles. This is part of the explanation of the strength of the Collins shot. He can crack a ball to the opposite wing with little apparent effort. When he aims at goal, it is like something out of a gun.

'Bobby's legs, as expected in one of his size, are short. That however, is an advantage rather than a handicap because the longer a footballer's legs are the more likely he is to be knocked off balance. Loss of balance is more than just loss of the split second that means so much. It puts added strain on the leg muscles. That means fatigue to be overcome.

'This matter of balance is important in other respects. Watch Bobby Collins beat an opponent. He does it quickly. He does it in little space. The bigger fellows can't do it that way. The smallness of Bobby's feet is another advantage. He takes size three and a half boots. He also has high insteps. This means he doesn't have to get his body over the ball to ensure accuracy of direction and trajectory.

'These things are all physical. There is a lot more in the make-up of Bobby Collins. For him a match doesn't end when the referee blows for full time, especially if Bobby's performance has failed to reach his own high standard. Bobby truly starts to prepare for a match as soon as the previous one ends. He goes to bed at what most people would consider a normal time in the early part of the week. On Thursday and Friday he is between the sheets by nine o'clock. In his earliest days he went to bed even earlier. Discipline like that obviously plays a big part in making Bobby an outstanding figure in big football.

'His advice to youngsters hoping to make a name in football is in keeping with his own way of living. "Football may be a game," says Bobby, "but a player has to work at it. When I was a youngster just starting, I played as often as possible and I trained hard. I have reaped the benefit since and can't offer any better advice." Work-train-play-think. There you have the ingredients of greatness. They have helped Bobby Collins to defy that often-quoted football saying that the good big 'un will always beat a good little 'un.'

At the turn of the year, Everton eased past Kings Lynn and Manchester City in the FA Cup but in the League just 1 win in 4 games resulted in the chairman calling a 'clear the air' meeting with the manager and players. Bobby recalled:

As captain I was first to receive his opinions and I was not happy when Mr Moores inferred that I wasn't giving my all. Nobody criticises my work rate, winning was everything to me. I was fuming and let him know. After the meeting without thinking I told a journalist the whole story. The next day I had a frank discussion with Mr Moores and told him if he didn't think I was giving everything he could get rid of me. I soon realised though how much the club meant to him. His critical words were aimed to get the team fired up again and we parted on good terms. By the weekend however my chat with the journalist was headline news. I apologised to the chairman

Bobby's story by cartoonist Tom Taylor.

because details of the team meeting should have stayed within the club, and credit to him, he realised that my actions were in the heat of the moment and that was the end of the matter.

Everton's next match was a crunch fifth-round clash against Burnley in the FA Cup. Bobby scored, but a 3-1 defeat resulted in the manager bringing in new players. Although he kept his place in a defeat at Nottingham Forest and helped his side defeat Wolves 4-0; the latter game would be Bobby Collins' last in Everton colours. Highly rated Blackpool 'keeper Gordon West had joined Everton and made his debut against Wolves and Bolton's Denis Stevens was earmarked for Collins' inside right slot. Bobby was not happy and decided it was time to move on when he was offered the chance to fight for a place on the right wing with Billy Bingham.

At the start of the campaign a knee ligament injury meant I was out for a month and it took time to regain my fitness, which was clearly not to the liking of the new boss. I'd been unsettled since Carey's departure and the atmosphere was changing.

Bobby leaves Merseyside with a win.

Everton ended the season fourth; their best finish since 1939 and ensuring European football for the first time, but for Bobby Collins new challenges lay ahead. His efforts though have not been forgotten on Merseyside. Everton legend Brian Labone: 'Bobby Collins made the biggest impact on me during my career. When I broke into the side on a regular basis in 1959, Bobby was skipper and the key player in the first team. Football coverage in the media during the 1950s was very different to now. Of course, I'd heard of Bobby because he was a Scottish international and had played for Celtic, but it wasn't until I saw him in training that I realised just how good he was.

'The first thing that struck me was that he had his own training method. One of his main attributes was that he was very quick off the mark. He kept this up by doing lots of sprints with his own spikes. Everton adopted his methods and it helped us all.

'Bobby was the ultimate professional. Johnny King and I used to chat a lot to him. We were spellbound by his stories and tips. He taught me a lot during the early stages of my career. I remember challenging him for a ball during a training match. I was over six foot, so you'd think it would be a mismatch going in against Bobby, but he went in hard and took me out. I was amazed by his strength, aggression and desire. Next time I went in a lot firmer and he said with a wry smile "you're learning son", but that was Bobby, no quarter was given on or off the pitch. I learned a lot from him.

'When I got into the first team we were in a bad position. During a difficult couple of seasons he kept us up and transformed Everton. Most sides had a Scot who brought a touch of iron to the side. Tottenham had Dave Mackay, we had Bobby and he got us out of trouble time and again. He also weighed in with crucial goals.

'Harry Catterick had a policy of selling players before their sell-by date. He usually got it right, but he got it wrong with Bobby Collins. At Leeds, Bobby went on to have a tremendous impact and when they got promotion we had some really tough battles. Leeds had a few fiery players such as Giles, Bremner and Hunter, and they were a physical side, but the team was badly treated by the press because they were a great side.

'Bobby had a heart the size of me and was one of the biggest stars of the era. If he was playing today, he'd be one of the biggest stars now. He was a tremendous player.'

Numerous clubs showed an interest in Bobby, including Don Revie at Leeds United, whose team was lying precariously at the foot of the Second Division.

Following Everton's defeat at Burnley I was told that Don Revie wanted to sign me. Les Cocker had been at the match and had recommended me to his manager. The two clubs agreed a fee of £25,000 and I was soon on my way after agreeing terms.

Don Revie recalled in *White Heat*: 'A journalist tipped me off that Everton might be willing to let Bobby go, so after we got confirmation of this from their manager, Harry Catterick, I travelled to Goodison the following morning, with two of our directors, to open negotiations. I spent an hour with Bobby after training and he told me in no uncertain terms that he felt that he still had a lot to offer as a First Division player, didn't fancy going to a club with one foot in the Third. We left it that he would think it over for a couple of days and get back to me. But as we headed for home, I decided to have another chat with him. I remember, we arrived at his house at 2 p.m. and waited in the car no less than five hours before he turned up. We didn't leave until 2.30 a.m. the next morning, but by that time, Bobby had agreed to join us.'

When Bobby Collins signed for Leeds on 8 March 1962, his new side was propping up the bottom of the table:

Bury P30 Pts 26, Bristol Rovers P32 Pts 25, Middlesbrough P30 Pts 24, Brighton P31 Pts 24, Charlton Athletic P28 Pts 22, LEEDS UNITED P31 Pts 22.

People questioned why I was joining a club struggling near the foot of the Second Division. The answer was simple; Don was very ambitious and believed they could be on the threshold of something big if they could avoid relegation. At the time the side had too many players nearing the 'veteran' age but he felt that I was the ideal person to guide the team to safety. I had nothing to lose because my career was going nowhere at Everton. After signing I drove home. During the evening I received a call from Bill Shankly who asked if it was true if I had signed for Leeds, which I confirmed. He said, in that case I wish you all the best. Bill was a top man.

TEN

STEPPING STONES
1962-1963

Bobby made his Leeds United debut against Swansea Town on 10 March 1962, and scored the opening goal in a 2-0 win. A defeat at Southampton was soon forgotten when a Bremner brace accounted for Luton Town. A hard-earned draw at Leyton Orient and win against Middlesbrough saw Leeds edge their way from the bottom of the table, but they were still far from safe and of concern to Don Revie, his new signing was becoming unsettled.

I was living in Aintree and travelled to Leeds for training. It wasn't ideal and in my haste to get away from Everton I thought maybe I should have joined a club closer to home. I had a long chat with Don and he persuaded me to give myself longer to settle. I agreed.

Don and I had the same outlook on how we should be playing. He wanted me to instil in the players a never-say-die attitude throughout a game. The defence had to tighten up and be disciplined at the back. I sat in the middle of the park, leaving four in attack, with the wingers coming back to help when necessary.

Don had been trying these tactics without success, but I made my point forcibly to the players that this would be our tactics come what may. Playing as a team was the key to survival. This way we would do no worse than draw, and hopefully snatch a win to avoid relegation.

The tactics were working but it was slow progress. Three consecutive 1-1 draws at Preston, Walsall and Bury were followed by stalemates against Bury and Derby County at Elland Road. One game now remained; a win at Newcastle United would guarantee safety.

We were confident because we'd only lost 1 of our last 10 games. The mood of the players was simply to get the job done.

Leeds were quickly off the mark and by half-time were able to relax having built up a 3-0 lead, courtesy of a Billy McAdams brace and an own goal. The second half saw Leeds hold on with some comfort. As results transpired, Bristol Rovers' defeat at Luton meant

Leeds were safe irrespective of the result at St James Park, but prior to kick-off they could not rely on such a scenario.

Eric Stanger wrote in the *Yorkshire Post*: 'Leeds United's escape from relegation was achieved with almost ridiculous ease. If Leeds had little to beat at least they did the job thoroughly and without fuss. They played calmly, as if they had not a care in the world and that they felt the result must inevitably go their way so long as they kept their heads.'

It was a very happy dressing room afterwards and I knew that with the number of youngsters about to come through, we would not be in this position again.

Bobby had made an immediate impact. In *Jack Charlton: The Autobiography*, his former teammate noted: 'Bobby played a vital part in ensuring that we stayed up in the Second Division. From then on the only way forward was up... What marked him out, and what made the difference to the Leeds sides he played in, was his commitment to winning. He was so combative; he was like a little lightweight boxer...

Leeds debut... and a goal to boot.

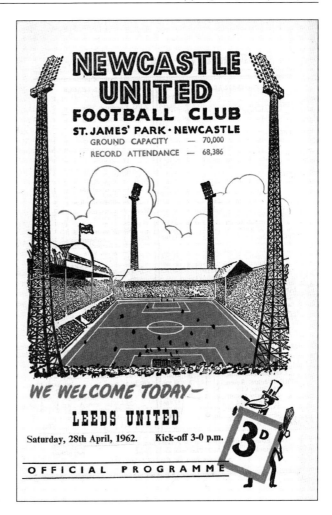

We're safe.

He introduced a sort of 'win at any cost' attitude in the team. Probably because we had a very young side at the time, the other players were very much influenced by his approach to the game.

'I got on all right with Bobby, but I didn't like to play against him. Even when we were playing five-a-side practice matches, you never knew what he was liable to do because he always wanted to win so much. But that was the attitude we needed at the time.

'Bobby introduced a much more professional attitude to winning. In the past we'd often score a goal but then let the other side back into it. Now we'd score a goal and that would be it. We'd lock it up and that was the end of the game. Our defence was rock-solid and we tackled hard. Nobody liked playing against us.

'Bobby might not have been captain, but in those early years he was the real leader of the team. He introduced a new spirit, which Don encouraged, "all for one and one for all".'

Star attraction.

Billy Bremner recalled in *Leeds United & Don Revie*: 'He never gave us a minute, because he was always telling us to do this, and do that, and do something else, and go tight there, and give it plenty of room in another place, and then get everybody running and running... Nobody who knew him can ever forget him, and the way in which he kept up our spirits when we'd been beaten, and was always saying there's another time, and knew it because he'd seen it before.'

There were no thoughts of relegation as the 1962/63 season unfolded, despite Leeds winning only 8 matches before Christmas. The return of former legend John Charles from Juventus didn't work, and he soon moved back to Italy. Instead Don Revie decided to bring in a number of his talented youngsters. Results slowly improved and Bobby Collins was the central figure to Revie's plans. After his performance in a hard-earned draw at Derby County, Phil Brown in the *Yorkshire Evening Post* observed: 'To borrow a phrase from Maurice Chevalier, thank heaven for little Bobby Collins. Without

Leeds United 1962/63. *From left to right, back row*: Mason, Charlton, Younger, Charles, Hair, Smith. *Front row*: Bremner, Storrie, Goodwin, Collins, Hawksby, Johanneson.

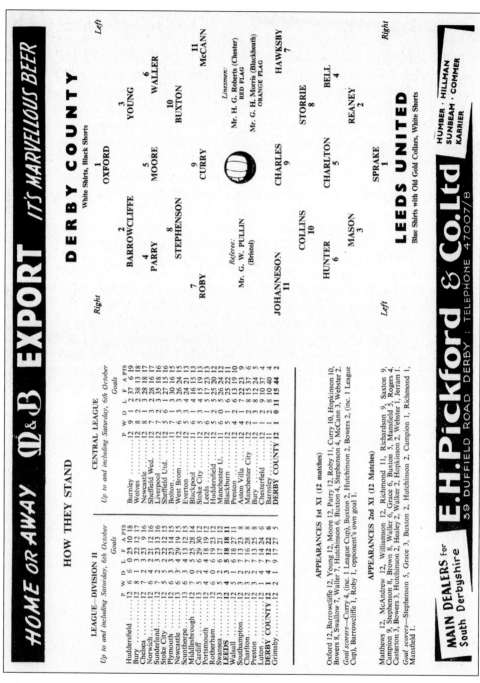

Bobby and the gentle giant, John Charles, team up.

Close call... Bobby's shot is saved by Norwich City 'keeper Lennon.

him I think the side would have been very ragged. The longer the game went the more ground he covered, and he was within a few yards of each byline in even the last two minutes.'

Bob Russell's *Daily Mirror* piece noted why Bobby was the complete player following his display in a 1-0 win against Newcastle United: 'Classy Collins... tantalising the Newcastle defence with a deft touch here and a defence-splitting through-ball there. Cannonball Collins... popping up suddenly in the penalty area and testing 'keeper Dave Hollins to the limit. Courageous Collins...letting his enthusiasm almost boil over when he 'had words' with tall Newcastle centre half George Thompson.' Edgar Turner in the *Sunday Mirror* agreed: 'Man of the Match for me was Bobby Collins. I think he is even better now than when he was with Everton. There was barely a blade of grass that he didn't either trample down as he scoured the field, or cut down with his beautiful ground passes. He was everywhere. Sometimes he was in situations with men looking almost twice his height, menacing him. But always Bobby came out with a big grin on his face.'

The pick of the pre-Christmas games was a 3-0 win over Norwich City and an impressive 6-1 win against Plymouth Argyle, Bobby grabbing his second goal of the season with a 30-yard special. The season however, was put on hold as the 'big freeze'

versus

PLYMOUTH ARGYLE

SATURDAY, 17th NOVEMBER, 1962

OFFICIAL PROGRAMME 4d

Six hitters... Bobby scores in a 6-1 win.

struck. There would be no games until March 1963. Once back in action results quickly picked up. Seven wins from 10 games saw Leeds shoot up the table. Suddenly promotion was a real possibility. The last three games of Leeds' purple patch brought a 4-1 victory at home to Preston and consecutive wins against Charlton Athletic during a hectic four-day spell in April, a month that saw Leeds play 9 League games. In the midst of all these matches Leeds enjoyed a reasonable run in the FA Cup. Their third-round clash was postponed twelve times due to the adverse weather, but when played Bobby opened the scoring in a 3-1 win against Stoke City. Following a 2-0 victory at Middlesbrough, Leeds eventually went out of the competition to Nottingham Forest.

Back in the League, a defeat at Portsmouth was soon forgotten as Leeds defeated Scunthorpe United, Cardiff City and Luton Town. Four games remained but after playing themselves onto the fringes of the promotion battle, three consecutive defeats, including a derby defeat at home to Huddersfield Town, ended their hopes. The loss to their West Yorkshire rivals was their first at Elland Road since October but Leeds had gone down fighting. Reporter Rex Traill commented: 'This was a rip-roaring derby. No

All white now!

holds were barred, there was good football and bad, harsh tackles and dainty stuff…never a dull moment.'

Leeds ended the season on a high with a 5-0 thumping of Swansea at Elland Road. Reporters were impressed. Jim Beecroft enthused in the *Sunday Mirror*: 'Leeds fans cheered and clapped their team off the field at the end of this nap hand as jubilantly as if they had just won the FA Cup. It was a well-deserved tribute to a remarkable season for a team, which must stand a very good chance of climbing back to the club's rightful place in the First Division next season. Revie's confident outfit can hardly wait for season 1963/4 to begin.' Graham Fisher added: 'I have never seen a team score five and look as exhilaratingly anxious for a sixth as Leeds United. The result and fifth place were settled long before the fifth goal. This team is a deafening echo of Revie's own enthusiasm, skill and unerring judgement of junior talent, and must be classic contenders for next year's promotion race.'

Revie's team had impressed everybody. Phil Brown of the *Yorkshire Evening Post* summed up the campaign: 'The season is ending at Elland Road in an almost rosy glow of hope about next season. For one that had to come from behind, and wade through an extra heavy backlog of frozen fixtures, the side has given us all a very good run for our money. The team, board and staff worked away on the field and off, and they have had their reward with the firm footing on which the club stands today. Don Revie's unsparing efforts to give the club the real nursery it has so long lacked lets one look forward to next August in optimism. Probably not all his youngsters will make it, no manager has ever had a 100 per cent return from his nursery, but he has quite a few who look racing certainties.' Regarding Bobby Collins' impact in his first full season, Brown noted: 'He has been the mainspring match after match, and a heck of a lot of improvement in the other players would not have taken place but for his unflagging work and his shrewd generalship.'

The club had turned the corner and the impact of Don Revie and Bobby Collins influenced first-team players and squad members alike. Norman Hunter recalled in *Biting Back*: 'In my book he is among the greatest players ever to have played for the club. In him we had one of the best players I have ever seen. He was an absolute cracker. He could hit short passes, long passes, tackle and score goals, and he was the bravest individual I ever came across. He had a great appetite for the game and wonderful vision. People have their own ideas of what the turning point was for Leeds back in the 1960s. Some would say the signing of Johnny Giles from Manchester United but there is no doubt in my mind that it was Revie's decision to bring Bobby to Elland Road. He came to keep us out of the Third Division and he did that and much more. He was awesome for a little fella… He was a great motivator and when he shouted out during games, 'Come on, get stuck in,' believe me, you did. He set the example and it seemed to carry on from there. Bobby epitomised Leeds United. He had this great will to win and it rubbed off on the rest of us.'

Tommy Henderson arrived from St Mirren in November 1962. He would stay for three years and typified the mood within the camp. 'I was immediately struck by the 'family' atmosphere at Elland Road. Being the same height and build as Bobby we naturally became close. When we were measured for club suits they would only measure one of us! During training, Bobby would do a lot of short sprint sessions. That was a key part to his game and of course he was so tough on the park. The five-a-sides were always a bit tasty, especially when we had the Scots against the English lads.

'Bobby's influence was immense and he was the centre of everything. Before a game he was always highly motivated, a real winner. At team talks Don used to say that if Bobby was free, give him the ball, run into space and he'd give you the return. Off the field, Don was in charge, but on it Bobby took over. He was brilliant to play with because of his footballing brain. Bobby could pick a pass out instantly; he also had a great shot and was 'bending' the ball well before anyone else became renowned for the skill. Bobby was the kingpin and nearly always the star man every week. In matches you could here players saying; "mark Collins". They knew that if they stopped him then that would stop Leeds playing, but generally they couldn't.

'When it comes to the great Leeds midfield players, people quite rightly talk about Billy Bremner and Johnny Giles, but I think Bobby was a better player overall. He had Billy's aggression and Johnny's passing accuracy, though not his two-footed ability. Bobby was a brilliant player and started everything off at Leeds. He was the best thing that happened to the club and the greatest signing the boss ever made.'

It was a great campaign overall for us. With youngsters like Gary Sprake, Paul Reaney, Norman Hunter and Billy Bremner settled in the side, more players in the youth team not quite ready to come through, Don was convinced there was tremendous potential. The mix was great because there was also experienced squad players and pros like Jack Charlton, Willie Bell and myself supporting. We also had Albert Johanneson who could destroy any defence.

ELEVEN

PROMOTION CHARGE
1963-1964

Leeds United began the 1963/64 campaign as one of the pre-season favourites, and got off to a fine start; winning their opening encounters at home to Rotherham and Bury. Following a draw at Rotherham, Revie's team lost a five-goal thriller at Manchester City. The defeat could not solely be attributed to their skipper's absence through injury, but it is no coincidence that on his return it heralded the start of an unbeaten 21-game run. He would not miss another League match during the season.

Following the 3-0 win against Bury, one reporter pondered how Leeds would fare without their charismatic skipper. 'Collins was the mainspring of a series of well-organised raids. For a player of his age, he showed astonishing energy and resolution. More than that, he showed his colleagues by sheer example the way to break down a sturdy defence. When Bury retreated as he gained possession in midfield and they waited for him to pass, Collins performed the unexpected. He suddenly saw a gap and from 30 yards fired the ball through it with such power that not even such an accomplished goalkeeper as Harker had a chance of preventing a goal.'

Slowly but surely the team gelled. A win at Portsmouth was followed by 3 draws. With new signing Johnny Giles, from Manchester United, settling, results improved. Leeds moved into the promotion frame with 5 consecutive wins. Bobby scored a penalty against Norwich City, at Northampton Town as Leeds notched a first away win of the campaign, and at Middlesbrough, according to reporter Ronald Crowther, a 'fantastic dipping drive from 35 yards while defenders stood fast-footed in amazement.'

Leeds cruised to a 4-1 win at Southampton, their 9th win of the season in 15 games. Reporter James Hastings noted: 'Mastermind was little Scottish inside-left Bobby Collins, who was forever prompting their movements yet also found time to give a hand to a defence, which has the best record in the Second Division. Southampton's wing halves were too inclined to play too far upfield and Collins took advantage of the extra room it gave him keeping his forwards supplied with a flow of perfect passes.'

A 2-0 win at Grimsby took Leeds to the top by 'non-stop determination, luck and skill in that order', according to David Nicholls. A dropped point at home to promotion rivals Preston was soon recovered with hard-fought victories over Leyton Orient, Swansea Town and Plymouth. Seventeen matches unbeaten; Leeds had completed half the campaign and were in control of their own destiny. With Bremner, Charlton, Bell and Hunter playing with assurance, Leeds had the look of winners, but the key was their skipper; guiding, cajoling and encouraging his charges forward with only one aim… promotion.

Following a 2-0 win at Orient just before Christmas, Phil Brown's *Yorkshire Evening Post* article commented: 'Collins hallmarked a glorious game with United's first goal from a free-kick. Yet, it was one of his 'specials'… a 25-yard riser with late swing deliberately applied, but this was the 'special' of all 'specials'. The pace on the ball and its late swing away would have done credit to Freddie Trueman at his fieriest.'

At the turn of the year Leeds' form suddenly dipped. A 2-0 defeat at Sunderland ended a 20-game unbeaten run and opened up the promotion battle. Leeds now had only a 1-point advantage over Sunderland and Preston. Outsiders for promotion were Charlton and Manchester City. The loss was part of an 11-match spell, which yielded just 3 wins, including a crucial one against outsiders Manchester City, and another 2-0 defeat, this time at Preston. Their interests in both domestic Cup competitions had ended with defeat at Manchester City in the League Cup and Everton following a bruising FA Cup fourth-round replay.

Leeds United, August 1963. *From left to right, back row:* Weston, Hunter, Madeley, Sprake, Bell, Bremner, Wright. *Front row:* Johanneson, Reaney, Collins, Lawson, Giles.

It was great playing against my former club. I had great memories, but I wanted to impress and let their manager know he had made a mistake in letting me go. I was soon in a battle with the guy that replaced me. He had a go at me and I retaliated. I should have been sent off, but the referee saw his challenge and let the incident pass. Everton may have gone on to win the title, but they had been in a battle. They also knew we were an emerging team.

One target remained... promotion. With goals at a premium, Don Revie had pepped up his attack with the signing of former England international Alan Peacock from Middlesbrough. It proved an inspired decision. Peacock scored on his debut in a 2-2 draw at Norwich and added balance to the team. The defeat at Deepdale had seen Leeds slip to second spot, ahead of Preston on goal average only, but the loss would be the last as Leeds suddenly rediscovered their early-season form in the final 10 games. The renaissance began with a 3-1 home win against Southampton. It was a crucial victory and brought relief to Leeds supporters who were beginning to wonder if their dream of top-flight football was slipping away.

Reporter Ronald Kennedy wrote: 'The City of Leeds, hungry for a taste of the First Division, breathed a sigh of relief in the 72nd minute of this rugged battle tinged with

The only way is up for Scots Bell, Storrie, Bremner, Henderson and Collins.

116

NORTHAMPTON TOWN

BRODIE

2
COCKCROFT

3
EVERITT

4
LECK

5
BRANSTON

6
MILLS

7
HAILS

8
KANE

9
LARGE

10
REID

11
LINES

Referee : W. M. HOLIAN
(Chesterfield).

Linesmen : J. CURTIN (Walsall).
(Red Flag)
R. D. HASTIE (Banbury).
(Yellow Flag)

JOHANNESON
11

COLLINS
10

STORRIE
9

WESTON
8

GILES
7

HUNTER
6

CHARLTON
5

BREMNER
4

HAIR
3

REANEY
2

SPRAKE

LEEDS UNITED

Another strike from Bobby as the promotion race gathers pace.

promotion glamour. Bobby Collins, a little chunkier and a little slower than in his heyday, swept away with the ball towards the left edge of the penalty area. Elland Road groaned because it looked a thousand to one that wee Bobby had thrown away a golden chance to settle the Saints' hash once and for all. But suddenly the little general's foot struck like the tongue of an angry vampire, and the ball tore savagely into the net. Till then, United, once a goal ahead and then level had dangled the nervous fans on the end of a thread of suspense.'

Bobby's strike would be his last of the season, but more importantly the victory was followed up with further 3-1 wins against Middlesbrough and Grimsby, sending Leeds back to the top, and proved the perfect tonic for 3 vital Easter wins in 4 games. Phil Brown in his *Green Post* column noted: 'We should be able to see the winning post after Easter, but not I think the winner. I reckon there is going to be a photo-finish.'

Leeds win a hard-fought match against Manchester City (© Photopress, Leeds).

Don Revie arranged overnight stops to ease the travelling between Newcastle, Derby and Leeds. Revie's planning paid off as his side won a tough encounter at Newcastle United, courtesy of goal from Giles, before picking up a point at Derby County. Following a days rest, Leeds won a hard-earned 2-1 victory in the return with Newcastle; Albert Johanneson scoring a brilliant winner.

Albert was some player on his day. Nobody could live with him. Against Newcastle he was surrounded by players, but side-step them all with a brilliant piece of skill before slipping the ball past the 'keeper as he raced from his line. It was some goal.

Four games now remained, and Leeds needing four points to secure promotion. A 2-1 win over Leyton Orient made the task simpler, although it was a far from convincing display. No Leeds United follower was complaining though.

Reporter Andrew Evans observed: 'Wee Bobby Collins, the canny Scots schemer whose gossamer-fine threads of intrigue have virtually sewn up a neat promotion package for Leeds, did it again yesterday. He may not have shone as a marksman in a game where moderate Leyton scarcely ever seemed likely to halt the Leeds promotion charge, but his wily generalling of his forwards left a true stamp of greatness on the match.'

Leeds travelled to Swansea Town needing just one point. A brace from Alan Peacock inside 20 minutes and a Giles strike before the interval sealed a return to top-flight football. With Sunderland drawing 0-0 at Southampton, only 1 point now separated Leeds from the Second Division title; forty years after their last triumph. Reporter Albert Barham commented: 'Leeds United, all grace and symmetry, snatched up an ailing Swansea team, swirled them round the Vetch Field and by winning 3-0 returned to the First Division. Collins, short, squat and with feet of almost tactile sensitiveness as he rolled the ball, smoothed it and plotted the downfall of Swansea, did as he pleased. Johnson could not subdue him, neither could Evans and when there were goals to score there was Peacock with a remarkable sleight of foot for a big man.'

Following the win Don Revie said: 'We want that championship flag to fly over the ground next season. We have a family spirit at Elland Road and everyone has been prepared to work that little bit harder and do that little bit extra. That has been shown on the field. The players have given 100 per cent effort in every game and no team, win, lose or draw can do more than that. Their obedience to orders, tactical and otherwise has been most gratifying and I know they have repeatedly lost the chance to make flattering headlines by making sure of victory or a point with unspectacular methods.'

Eric Stanger of the *Yorkshire Post* was in no doubt who the driving force had been: 'Collins' generalship and leadership have been decisive factors in taking Leeds back into the First Division. Few inside forwards work harder than Collins and generally they are a hard-working race, they have to be in the modern game. Few players can strike such a response from their colleagues. His influence both in the dressing room and on the field has been incalculable.'

Don had taken some crates of champagne along and we celebrated on the journey home by train. It was a very satisfying journey back to Leeds. All the talk throughout the season was how good Sunderland were. We were determined to finish above them.

Disappointingly, Leeds failed to clinch the title in their final home game of the season against Plymouth. They thanked their supporters prior to the 1-1 draw in a lap of honour, but the point gained meant a victory in the last game at Charlton Athletic was now required to claim the championship trophy. Leeds duly claimed the crown, courtesy of a Peacock brace. Revie's team received rave reviews:

Roy Horobin's view in the *Sunday Express* was: 'Leeds looked every inch a championship side in this their last match. Superbly confident Leeds were in charge right from the kick off. Two little 'uns, inside left Bobby Collins and left half Billy Bremner, and a big 'un, centre half Jack Charlton, were perhaps the brightest stars in this great Leeds side. Linkmen Collins and Bremner dominated the middle of the field.'

Another national paper wrote: ' "Champions Champions" chanted the Leeds supporters, and how the Yorkshire side lived up to the honour. Leeds crushed Charlton to take the

Second Division title back to Leeds for the first time since 1924. The First Division will surely welcome these lion-hearted fighters. No one deserved greater credit than tiny Bobby Collins, who returns to his rightful place in top-grade soccer. He inspired Leeds with a display of control and precision passing which mesmerised the Charlton defence.'

The *Yorkshire Post's* reporter commented: 'It was United's solid teamwork which carried them through at Charlton just as it has done so many times this season. If United had a star it was once more Collins, a fine captain and inside left. Once more he covered the field. He had energetic and clever support from Bremner at right half but United's defenders were so good and so willing to assist their eager forwards, that backs Reaney and Bell must each have made half a dozen sorties into attack.'

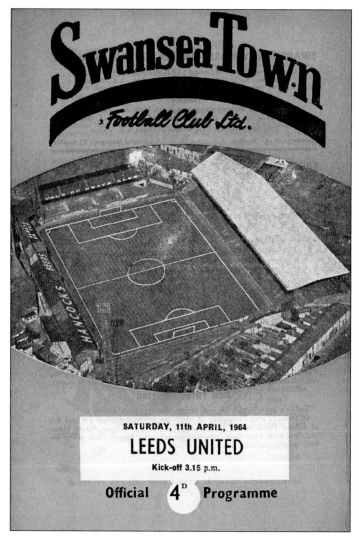

Top-flight football here we come!

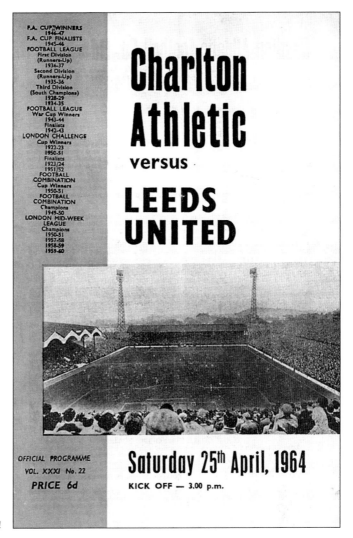

Job done!

Don Revie told the *Yorkshire Post*: 'I am glad we have won the championship for the player's sake. They certainly deserve it. When you think of it, it has been a fantastic performance to go through the season with only 3 League defeats. All credit to the boys. They have trained hard, worked hard on the field and carried out their instructions to the letter.'

As for his skipper, Revie told Arthur Walmsley of the *Sun*: 'In the first season I took over at Leeds we were heading for the Third Division. Crowds had dropped to 8,000 but with 11 matches to go I went out and made the best buy of my life, Bobby Collins. There were rumours that he had a bad knee and that at 31 he was on his way out. I had him medically examined and he proved fully fit. That was enough for me, I didn't doubt his ability. If there is a better inside forward in Great Britain, I'd like to see him. He's one of the all-time greats.'

Leeds set a number of records. The only First or Second Division team to complete the season with only three defeats, 63 points was the highest number of Second Division points gained since the war. In addition, Leeds had completed a season without being beaten at home for the first time and created three new longest sequences by United teams. An unbeaten League run of 20 matches during the campaign was the best since 1927/28, a term when another United side gained promotion. Eight consecutive away wins, and 10 unbeaten away matches, also set new standards.

Everybody was thrilled that we'd made it back into the First Division and we couldn't wait to test ourselves. I knew we had a good side, despite many of the team not having played top-flight football, and would not struggle. I was also delighted for our supporters. They had not seen success like this for a long time and lapped it up.

One of the keys to our success was team spirit and the tremendous banter during training, although Scotland v. England clashes got a bit too tasty. When you look at

Heroes' welcome during an open top celebration through Leeds City Centre.

Second Division Champions. *From left to right, back row*: Bell, Reaney, Goodwin, Sprake, Williamson, Hunter, Lawson. *Front row:* Giles, Bremner, Storrie, Collins, Revie (manager), Weston, Greenhoff, Charlton.

the line-ups it's not that surprising. The Scottish side would include Billy Bremner, Jim Storrie, Willie Bell, Eddie Gray, Peter Lorimer and myself. As for England, Jack Charlton, Paul Reaney, Terry Cooper, Paul Madeley and Norman Hunter would line up.

In one of the first 'friendly' clashes we told the English lads what we would do to them in the dressing room prior to going down to a 5-0 defeat! We were not happy, and got serious. We proceeded to win the next few clashes, but the tackles were getting tastier by the game until Les Cocker stopped the fixture.

So Scotland v. England clashes were banned, but the boss went out of his way to keep us occupied between games, and it was during this period that the regular bingo sessions started. Some people criticised Don, but it did avert the boredom on our travels and helped build a tremendous bond between the players. We all had a pleasant close-season break.

TWELVE

DOUBLE HEARTACHE
1964-1965

A fortnight before the start of the new season, the football authority's magazine *FA News* published a list of clubs with the worst disciplinary record the previous term. Leeds United headed it. Before a ball had been kicked accusations of dirty play and over-professionalism dogged them. The report though was inaccurate and if pundits had studied the full list of offending players, they would have noted that the majority of offending Leeds players were juniors and reserves, not first team players. The damage, however had been done. Playing against Don Revie's Leeds would not be a place for the faint-hearted.

The press called us cynical and ruthless, but what they didn't comment on was the fact that opposing players were determined to intimidate us. Also not every player

Leeds United 1964/65. *From left to right, back row:* Bell, Hunter, Reaney, Charlton, Greenhoff, Cooper. *Middle row:* Owen (coach), Peacock, Lawson, Sprake, Revie (manager), Williamson, Madeley, Wright, English (physio). *Front row:* Bremner, Giles, Storrie, Collins, Henderson, Weston, Johnson.

Cartoon capers by *Yorkshire Evening Post* cartoonist Speed.

had the make-up of players such as Stan Matthews or Tom Finney. My philosophy was always to give as good as I got; if someone kicked me I'd instinctively kick back. It was certainly tasty at times because no quarter was given or expected. It was not pretty to watch at times, but it took courage and guts to deal with, not to mention a fair amount of skill. The game was for hard men and we were up to the task.

Leeds made a confident start to the season. Winning their opening three games against Aston Villa, Liverpool and Wolves, Revie's boys served notice that they would not roll over.

After the win at Villa Park, Eric Stanger in the *Yorkshire Post* commented: 'Leeds United gave every indication in their first game that diligence and industry will enable them to meet their rent without much fear of ejection. United's tactics were those which served them so well last season; close marking, hard tackling to which no one could take exception on this occasion, and a smothering defensive cover when danger threatened their goal. It was effective rather than spectacular and too much for Villa.' As for the Leeds skipper, Stanger observed: 'Collins, still from the stand looking like a schoolboy who has strayed into a grown-ups game, was as ever an inspiration and a

Back in the big time!

comfort to his colleagues. If there was a hole to be filled because a man had either strayed or been drawn out of position Collins filled it. His capacity for work was enormous and he was desperately unlucky not to score with one of his characteristic 'banana' shots.'

Frank McGhee of the *Daily Mirror* echoed the opinion of many observers after the defending champions Liverpool had been beaten: 'Leeds lost what they were most anxious to get rid of, a reputation for too much vigour, too much defence and not enough attacking ideas. They certainly had far too much swift striking power for the Liverpool defence, which last season boasted the best record in the First Division. I have never seen them so often rattled, so easily riddled as they were last night by a Leeds team that still plays this game furiously, but on this evidence, has temperament on a tight reign.'

Though 3 of the next 6 encounters ended in defeat, the heaviest at Blackpool, 7 consecutive victories moved Leeds into title contention. After a fine 3-1 win over Tottenham Hotspur, Phil Brown in the *Yorkshire Evening Post* noted the impact of Leeds' talisman. 'Collins preserved his game and his generalship against the talent and experience of Spurs, and kept United's game simple, direct and to the point.'

Bobby scored in a 4-1 win against Sheffield United. The 'derby' was a raucous affair. Brian Eastham commented: 'The game had everything expected from a clash between two razor-sharp teams. One man was booked and one sent off, a penalty was saved and there were fouls galore.' The headlines though were nothing compared to those following Leeds clash at Everton when both teams were ordered off the pitch to calm down. James Mossop's *Sunday Express* piece read: 'Football flared up in some of the wildest, angriest scenes soccer has ever seen at Goodison Park... It all happened to a background of cascading missiles and ugly threats... a clash of two teams on big bonuses and an interest in First Division honours.' Edgar Turner's *Sunday Mirror* report did not disagree: 'Cassius Clay should have been refereeing this match, with Sonny Liston running one of the lines. A few rhymes from the lip might have stopped tempers letting rip, and who wouldn't scare under Liston's glare?'

The clash at Goodison was one of the most ferocious games I ever played in for Leeds. The tackles were flying in and a section of fans threw their cushions on the field. The media blamed us, but some of the Everton players were going over the top time and again. The referee lost control. It was nasty and at times brutal. There were some horrendous challenges that day, but it was not in our nature to turn the other cheek. The goal was crucial. I took a free kick and flipped one in... boomph, Willie Bell

Leeds defeat the defending champions 4-2.

Seaside blues! TV stars Mike and Bernie Winters entertain the Leeds team prior to a clash with Blackpool. The smiles soon disappeared after a 4-0 defeat. *From left:* Les Cocker, Billy Bremner, Mike Winters, Don Revie, Bernie Winters, Bobby Collins and Harry Reynolds.

scored with a header. A war of words followed, but eventually the dust settled. We knew though that every game from then on would be judged more intensely than ever.

Next up was Arsenal and Bobby was the key to a 3-1 win as Leeds moved into third spot 2 points adrift of League leaders Manchester United.

Derek Wallis put it thus in the *Daily Mirror*: 'Skipper Bobby Collins shook his fist angrily at the Leeds United defence and bellowed "Don't mess about with it"...or words to that effect! Words and action on inside left Collins' part made all the difference to a team that seemed to be suffering from inferiority complex against a highly competent Arsenal team. He followed up his verbal admonition by assuming control of both defence and attack, playing deep when necessary but always around when the forwards needed his assistance. I've heard of players taking matches by the scruff of the neck before, but rarely of one who assumed so much responsibility in any situation with complete authority.'

Another 4-1 victory, this time over Birmingham City had journalists drooling, such as Philip Pierce in the *Sunday Express*: 'Here was the power and the glory which proved beyond any doubt they are worthy of their lofty spot near the top of the form. They played it with the gentility and finesse of guests at a vicar's tea party. If all this seems one-sided, well that's how it was. Breathtaking Leeds had just about everything. There was the rock of steadiness of Jack Charlton and the daring and dash of Billy Bremner. There was the arrogant generalship of Bobby Collins, and there was the flashing genius of Albert Johanneson, the wing wizard.'

Despite a defeat at West Ham, wins against West Brom, Manchester United, Aston Villa and Wolves meant Leeds were joint leaders at Christmas. The victory at Old Trafford ended an unbeaten run of 19 games for the title favourites. Despite increasing fog, Leeds came through with a second-half strike from Bobby. It was touch and go though for Revie's team, who defended magnificently, as referee Jim Finney, 11 minutes from time, halted the game for seven minutes, before allowing the game to conclude.

Frank Clough wrote of the victory in the *Sun*: 'In a split second that is still captured in the deep-freeze of memory Bobby Collins made a major contribution to English soccer. He scored a goal and it carried a greater, deeper significance than even this shrewd and stocky Scot realised. It narrowed the point's gap at the top of

Ex-teammates Brian Labone and Bobby depart from the 'Battle of Goodison'.

the First Division and that means fiercer, keener and more intense competition in the future, which in turn means more excitement and entertainment for the paying public. It proved conclusively that Leeds, smeared as a dirty, roughhouse side are worthy of a place in the First Division and worthy of more support from their half-million population. And it showed to the world that this Manchester United team of all-stars can be beaten. Thank heavens Bobby didn't think of all these things as he drew his foot back. The weight of such responsibility might have made him miss!'

Edgar Turner echoed these words in the *Sunday Mirror*: 'Make no mistake about it; this was Leeds United's hour of true glory. Soccer's new young tearaways have snapped their jaws into the flanks of Matt Busby's wounded warriors. They had smashed 'invincible' Manchester United to defeat. They had tamed the most lethal attack in British football today and they have done it with a tremendous display of courage and fighting spirit.' Bobby told reporters:

We could see well enough, even when the referee called it off, but I felt sorry for some of the spectators. The goal... it began with Johnny, then to Billy and eventually to me from Terry Cooper. I hit it just right, exactly right. Ten yards range. It was a great feeling to see that ball sailing in... smashing. Some of the supporters probably didn't see it, but it was a terrific result, a great day all round.

Leeds had served notice that they were well and truly back in the big time, a point noted by Manchester United's Denis Law in an *Evening Times* article. Bobby's former Scotland teammate was also full of praise with the influence and form of Leeds United's skipper: 'Captaincy has, I think, been good for Bobby Collins. On the field today he is very much the general. All the time he is encouraging his team, urging them on, dictating the pattern. He wants the ball all the time, wants to dictate the style. His is flash and bustle, a wee pirate of a man. To look at Bobby Collins you'd expect him to play it close, delicate flicks and the like. Yet I know of no one who makes better use of the long ball to the wing. He can hit them too. Part of his secret is that he combines the long and the short ball so well that you never quite know what to expect. He is not as fast as he used to be, but he compensates for this with added experience and skill. Today I would rate him in the top six inside forwards in Britain.'

Law's manager, Matt Busby, was similarly impressed with his former player in the national side. He wrote in the *Scottish Daily Express*: 'Whenever I see Bobby Collins of Leeds United, I realise that the little 'un can still be a giant on the field. The wee inside forward has more than any Leeds player to lift the club from the depths of the Second Division to the heights of the First. He looks a happy player. He is always a tremendous worker, he paces it well, he is inspiring to younger players and patient with them, too. If young players are impetuous, he calms them down with a word of advice. If they need pepping up, he will do that nicely too. Bobby shirks nothing; they never come too big for him, but it is his football brain that makes him invaluable. He see things before they happen as all great players do, or he changes the face of a game

ARSENAL v. MANCHESTER UNITED — SATURDAY 28th NOVEMBER 1964
Denis Law hammers home a pass from Charlton (second from left) for United's first goal. At half time United led 3-0 but a tremendous rally by Arsenal in the second half reduced the arrears to 3-2 at the final whistle.
Photo by courtesy of The Sunday Express

Swinging Sixties…
Busby's boys are beaten.

with one sharp move. Other players have made a tremendous impact on their clubs by skill, personality and loyalty, but for sheer one-man impact, few have done so much as the lad who looks like a little imp on the pitch… Bobby Collins, Scotland's gift to Leeds United.'

A 1-1 draw with Blackburn on Boxing Day was followed up by a 2-0 win at Ewood Park. Derek Hodgson enthused in the *Daily Express*: 'On a night raw enough to keep Wenceslas at home Leeds finished their merriest Christmas with a victory that makes them joint kings of the First Division. Live, lean Leeds were twice as nimble as Rovers on a heavily sanded, frost-bound pitch. Their footwork apart, they won for the reason that has become so familiar to First Division clubs. Leeds will do twice as much work in half as much time as almost any other team.'

Two days into the New Year and Leeds reached the summit following a 2-1 win over Sunderland. Philip Pierce marked the occasion in the *Sunday Express*: 'Leeds, magnificent, superb Leeds, surged to the top of the table with a power display that filled Yorkshire hearts with bursting pride. Bobby Collins and his merry men were in devastating mood.

They used the ball with the same deft precision a surgeon wields his scalpel, mercilessly carving up punchless, spiritless Sunderland. Only the scoreline tells a lie.'

Leeds finally led the way, but only one hard-fought 2-1 victory at Arsenal would come their way in the next six League games, although they did remain unbeaten as they ground out results to keep them in what was now a three-way title race between Leeds, Manchester United and Chelsea. After a 0-0 draw at Tottenham, Sam Leitch of the *Sunday Mirror* noted: 'All he needed out there on the White Hart lane pitch was a mortar board and gown, perhaps even a blackboard on the centre spot. Then the stage would have been complete for Professor Bobby Collins, Master of Football, as he cursed and coaxed, finger-wagged and back-slapped his willing Leeds pupils to yet another precious point in the First Division championship race.'

Throughout this run, Leeds had moved into the quarter-finals of the FA Cup, where they would face Crystal Palace, after accounting for Southport, Everton and Shrewsbury. The last eight was the furthest the club had ever been in the competition, and that was a solitary appearance in 1950 against Arsenal. The clash against Everton was a classic. Leeds eventually came through in the replay at Goodison Park 2-1. Phil Brown complimented both Collins and Revie in the *Yorkshire Evening Post*: 'Leeds is today nearer to becoming one of the soccer cities of England than it has ever been. A brilliant young manager, who is making fools of his critics, and a very gallant side kicked their club's sad cup record in to the dustbin last night in foggy Liverpool by firmly

That'll do nicely for Harry Reynolds, Bobby and Don Revie... Southport in the FA Cup.

outplaying Everton's expensive collection of stars. In passing, the Scottish selectors must be all sorts of rude words not to re-recognise the way Collins is playing. He positively inflicted himself on his old club.'

It was a superb win. Jack Charlton was immense and scored a great goal, also Gary Sprake made up for his mistake in the first game with some great saves when required.

Collins was at his virtuoso best, and used all his experience to snuff out Shrewsbury's challenge. Bob Russell's comment in the *Daily Mirror*: 'Collins in this "somebody's got-to-show 'em" mood tamed Shrewsbury with a single-handed display that would have wrecked ordinary opposition. Five times he hit high velocity drives from all of 30 yards. Twice the ball swerved wide, once the crossbar quivered and twice the post took the impact. On the third occasion Collins hit the woodwork Johanneson hammered in the rebound.'

In a hard-fought encounter at Selhurst Park, Leeds' experience eventually came through with three second-half goals to record a fine 3-0 win to move into the semi-finals of the competition for the first time in the club's history. Phil Brown's words in the *Yorkshire Evening Post* were: 'With all these youngsters in the side I doubt if the team really appreciate yet what they have done to soccer in Leeds in getting themselves just ninety minutes from Wembley. The game went pretty well as I expected, physically very hard, legally or illegally, with United's superior class and discipline telling in the end with three second-half goals and their defence keeping out all Palace's far from clever attempts to get through.'

Technically we played well. Palace tried to get at us, but they had no chance of out-muscling us. If sides wanted a battle we had the players who could do so. It was a very satisfying win.

Back to League action, and Leeds drew with Fulham then faced a tricky clash at Burnley. The build up was meticulous as ever, or so Don Revie thought at an overnight stop in Harrogate. Bobby recalled in an interview.

The spirit was superb at Leeds and we always prepared well, but we got up to our share of antics. Before the clash at Turf Moor a prank went horribly wrong. Big Jack was the intended victim, but he spotted me before I was able to drench him and was off like lightning with me in tow armed with a bucket of water. His escape was a glass door, but as he flicked it back I went straight through it. The lads were all laughing at the escapade until they saw my arm. Les Cocker arrived, not pleased, and promptly took me to a local hospital to receive nine stitches in the gash. Don was not happy. He understood the lads needed to let off steam, but the accident was preventable and made sure we knew it! The injury was strapped and we beat Burnley 5-1. I grabbed two goals and received a wry smile from Don as if to say you're nearly forgiven!

Leeds are through to the last semi-finals.

A 4-1 win followed over Everton. James Mossop was loud in his praise in the *Sunday Express*: 'Football from the hipflask… warm and mature. Football to make you forget the bitter snowstorm, the squelching mud and the old-time friction that once gave these sides a bad name.' Leeds now took on Manchester United in the club's first ever FA Cup semi-final as Liverpool squared up to Chelsea. At Hillsborough, the two Pennine rivals served up a "dour, punishing game" according to Tom Holley of the *People*. James Mossop of the *Sunday Express* was damning: 'The vulgar thumpings of the game's lowest tactics wrecked what could have been a soccer symphony. There was kicking, butting, punching, shirt-tearing and every other evil football action to make Hillsborough hell.' Clive Toye's *Scottish Daily Express* piece read similarly: 'Manchester United and Leeds can take their tempers into a dark room and kick and punch and butt and spit at each other until summertime for all I care. They must learn, however, not to do it in their no-scoring English Cup semi-final. I am appalled that two of the teams we delightedly place among the country's fabulous four should behave like back-street delinquents in front of a semi-final crowd.'

The first game was a bit naughty, but that was caused by them; they started things, but typical of the media at the time Manchester did not receive the criticism that we would have for employing similar tactics. There were a number of unsavoury incidents, the worst when Big Jack and Denis Law clashed. Billy and Pat Crerand got involved in the mix and it set the tone of the game. It was a terrible pitch and a really tough match. We were second best before half-time but had the edge in the second half. At the end I was convinced we would win the replay.

The replay was totally different as a spectacle where Billy Bremner's late winner secured a first cup final for Leeds as a city celebrated. It had been close though, and for long periods it seemed that Busby's side would win. Leeds' resolve was total though, and gaining strength, entered the final stages and claimed a memorable win.

Eric Stanger wrote in the *Yorkshire Post*: 'Leeds rallied magnificently to win. The first half was even but Manchester United, playing at their brilliant best, stormed in with

Wembley here we come!

My ball… Bobby wins possession against West Ham as the title race hots up.

attack after attack for the first half-hour of the second half, only to be met by a Leeds defence which tackled unflinchingly and covered with rare skill, finally to weather the storm. Then almost picking themselves off the canvas they showed that unquenchable spirit which has carried them so far this season. Manchester were thrown back on their heels by the fierceness of the counter-attacks by this side that refused to be beaten. In that exciting last 15 minutes Leeds were right on top and Bremner's goal, the result of quick thinking as well as being brilliantly taken, won them the day.'

Eric Todd had kind words for Bobby and the team in the *Guardian*: 'No praise can be too high for Leeds. They are not a classic side, and will never satisfy the purists, but they have a wonderful team spirit and an outstanding captain in Collins, who rallied his side continuously… In the final analysis however, I think teamwork was the deciding factor.'

Don Revie was exultant: 'My proudest moment in my career was when the whistle went last night and Leeds United were in the final. Manchester played some absolutely scintillating football. I thought we were going to crack and we were certainly lucky not to go two down but we came through it, and according to my instructions, if there was still no score, Jim Storrie switched to the right wing and Bremner moved into the attack. It might not have come off, but it did. What pleased me most was that Leeds kept their heads.'

The replay was really something and the boys were just magnificent. As for the goal, I was going to take the free-kick but Johnny insisted on taking it, and of course Billy headed it in for the winning goal. After the game the atmosphere in the dressing room was wonderful. Of course we were relieved, but we also knew we were going to Wembley to play in the cup final; there is no better feeling. This was the first time the club had achieved it, it was brilliant. Everyone connected with the club was just so happy. We stayed at Grantham overnight; it was a terrific evening. I had to carry my roommate to bed!

Leeds went back to League action and capturing the moment following a fortuitous 2-1 win over West Ham, Max Jessop of *The People* noted: 'Leeds for the Championship, Leeds for the cup, Leeds, if their incredible luck holds out, for the Derby, the next General Election and the 1966 Boat Race.'

Pundits began to speculate whether tiredness was catching up on Revie's team with just seven League games remaining. Not so, as Stoke City and West Brom were defeated. However, the latter clash was the start of a six-match sequence in fourteen days that would settle the destiny of the title. Next on the agenda was a potential championship decider against Manchester United. One strike proved crucial in the home side's defeat. Eric Todd of the *Guardian* wrote: 'Revenge no less than victory was

Leeds lose a crunch match against Manchester United.

Simply the best!

very sweet and timely for the men from Old Trafford. Leeds were very disappointing… only Collins lived up to his reputation.'

For the Leeds skipper, the disappointment was great but he was soon celebrating after being named Footballer of the Year, the first Leeds United player, and Scot, to receive the most prestigious individual honour in English football. It was a fitting tribute to his impact at Elland Road, and quite unthinkable when he first arrived at the club. The progress had been stunning. Reporter Ken Lawrence commented: 'Was there any other choice? I think not. An Everton reject three years ago, Don Revie signed him for the bargain price of £25,000, he has steered Leeds from the very foot of the Second Division to the other end of the rainbow. He has won his place back in the Scotland team, commanded Leeds to become the Team of the Year. Now the Wee Fellow is to receive the statuette that places him on the roll of honour that marks the number one player of the year. For Bobby Collins, then, the climax to a wonderful season.'

Winning the Footballer of the Year award was very special. I was the first Scot to be awarded the honour, and when you consider Scots like Denis Law never won the award, it puts into perspective what it meant to me. It remains one of my fondest memories as a professional footballer.

Leeds travelled to Sheffield Wednesday without their inspirational skipper. Following a 3-0 drubbing Alan Thompson of the *Daily Express* noted. 'Like a ship without a rudder, Leeds without Bobby Collins foundered hopelessly even on the last lap of their title chase.' Leeds defeated Wednesday in the Easter return twenty-four hours later and Sheffield United in the penultimate match of the season, but Manchester United were now in control. Bobby was now back in the side, but a 3-3 draw at Birmingham in his side's final game, coupled with Manchester United's 3-1 win over Arsenal, meant the title would go to Old Trafford. Don Revie commented: 'Five days before a cup final, they are three goals down and fight back to draw 3-3. What more can any manager ask of his players?'

Leeds had enjoyed the best League campaign in the club's history and finished with the highest number of points by a First Division runner-up. Busby's team lost their final game of the season at Aston Villa, but they had clinched the title by virtue of a better goal average.

Five days on Leeds were ready for the FA Cup final, the first time a match involving Leeds would be live on television. Supporters would finally experience the 'razzamatazz' of a cup final.

It had been quite a season for the Leeds United skipper, who featured in numerous pre-match articles. Frank McGhee, *Daily Mirror*, summed up his attributes and impact in the players' cup final brochure *The Triumphant Year*:

'Off the field I look down on Bobby Collins…literally. On the field I look up to him in every way. That was the reason why I helped to make him Footballer of the Year in 1965. Leeds are very significant powers in the land today and this little man is one very big reason why. He is sergeant-major, captain and general in their army, this scaled down Hercules who was signed from Everton for only £25,000. I doubt if any club in post-war years has made a bigger mistake than Everton or a better bargain than Leeds that day. For their money they bought experience, ability, leadership, knowledge, courage all wrapped up in one neat tidy package, only five feet three inches high, weighing only 10 stone 2 pounds, but every inch and every ounce is class. Maybe Everton thought he was over the hill. If so it was one hell of a high hill because Bobby Collins still has a long way to travel before he will rank as a has-been in anyone else's book. He even forced Scotland to recall him to their international side at the age of 34, after six seasons in the cold. His performances for Leeds made them recognise and realise that in this player who combines tremendous strength, drive and determination with inch-perfect accuracy, they have someone who can still be a potential world-beater.'

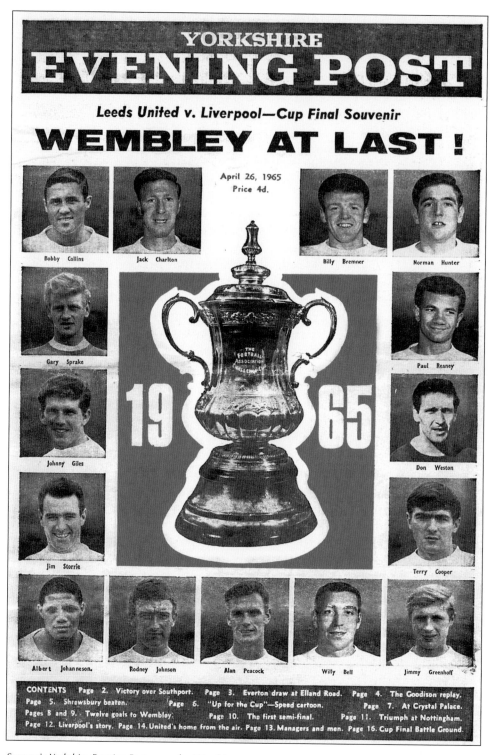

Souvenir *Yorkshire Evening Post* paper for Wembley.

Leeds United *v.* Liverpool, FA Cup final

Leeds United: Sprake, Reaney, Bell, Bremner, Charlton, Hunter, Giles, Storrie, Peacock, Collins, Johanneson
Liverpool: Lawrence, Lawler, Byrne, Milne, Yeats, Stevenson, Callaghan, Hunt, St John, Smith, Thompson

The television schedule was in marked contrast to today's blanket coverage:

BBC TV: 11.30 Danny Blanchflower shows viewers around the Wembley dressing rooms. 12.35 Recording of Stanley Matthews testimonial match. 2.10 How the teams reached Wembley. 3.00 The match, commentator Kenneth Wolstenholme.

ATV: 12.50-1.20 Eamon Andrews recalls great cup finals of the past ten years. Peter Lorenzo introduces celebrities. 2.40 The cup final, commentators Gerry Loftus and Jimmy Hill.

Third Network: 2.05 Brian Moore looks back. 2.45 The match, commentators Brian Moore, Alan Clark and John Camkin.

I preferred woollen to nylon because I felt more comfortable; the only trouble was that with constant washing they turned yellow. Throughout the campaign I'd worn my yellowing socks and for the final we had bright new white ones, which I was not happy about. After explaining this to Don, being incredibly superstitious himself, he insisted I wear my old discoloured socks that had served me so well during the season. I thought that would be the end of the matter, but the media picked it up and even the Duke of Edinburgh noticed them and pointed it out when he was introduced to the teams before the game!

Sadly, it was not to be as Liverpool broke Leeds hearts. In a dour game, during normal time chances were few. Liverpool full-back Gerry Byrne dislocated a shoulder following a clash with Bobby and Jim Storrie spent most of the game a passenger after picking up an injury. The game sprung into action during extra time after Roger Hunt had headed home a Byrne cross. Leeds fought back with a classic strike from Billy Bremner, but Liverpool claimed the win with an Ian St John header nine minutes from time.

Edgar Turner was not amused in the *Sunday Mirror*: 'For 90 goalless minutes it was a match of too many Marlon Brandos and not one Sir Laurence Olivier; too much method, not enough individual brilliance. It was drab and dismal. Stanley Matthews at fifty could have brought a bit more colour. Then this Wembley classic exploded. Liverpool for so long on top were not to be denied. Leeds were on defence for most of the match and their fans, who had already seen the League Championship slip away, watched sadly as the cup evaded them, too.'

His colleague Sam Leitch was also unimpressed: 'Ee-aye-addio, what a cup final dish to set before the Queen, a blundering ballet of inferior football saved from full stinker status by the first Wembley extra-time for eighteen years. Three goals in those extra 30 minutes rescued soccer's showpiece from being the gigantic £89,000 Flop of the Season. And it gave the Cup to Liverpool who deserved it most. At least Leeds showed

Right: Captain Fantastic!

Below: The players' cup final brochure.

Cartoon cup frolics by *Yorkshire Evening Post* cartoonist Speed

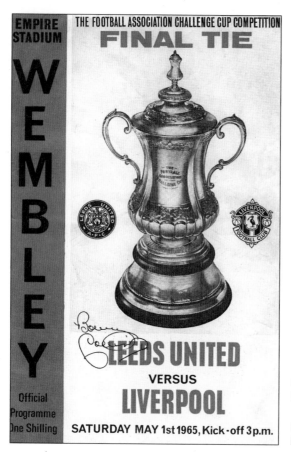

Left: A day barely believable when Bobby arrived at Leeds United.

Below: Cartoon fun as a city awaits the big day.

Above: Cup final line up. *From left to right, back row:* Hunter, Charlton, Sprake, Reaney, Bell. *Front row:* Giles, Storrie, Peacock, Revie (manager), Collins, Johanneson, Bremner.

Overleaf: The teams enter Wembley Stadium.

the courage, which manager Don Revie has pumped into them all season. Alas, the adrenalin worked for such a short period.'

James Mossop of the *Sunday Express*: 'For Leeds the final was a bitter disappointment. Everything they stand for, spirit, aggression and all-out enthusiasm, faded before Liverpool's well-drilled Reds. Leeds were pale phantoms of weeks ago when they would take on anyone with confidence and assurance.'

Eric Cooper had some sympathy for Leeds in the *Daily Express*: 'The saddest sight of any FA Cup final is the last walk of the losers as they leave the pitch and the glory to their conquerors. Nothing can change that, for whatever glamour of qualifying for Wembley it cannot obliterate the disappointment of failure when nearness has raised hopes to the skies. But if ever a team deserved special medals to match their outsize hearts it is Leeds, my team of the season, even though they still cannot boast a major triumph in their forty-five-year history. There will always be winners in the FA Cup or the League Championship, but never has a team come so near to winning both and won neither. Despite their disappointment of 'letting the fans down' their achievements must rank with those of Manchester United and Liverpool when you take into consideration this was their first season back in the First Division. Leeds scored a record number of points for title runners up and still only lost the title on goal average.

Then, within six days, they took the previous champions to extra time in the first extended cup final in eighteen years.'

Don Revie commented: 'The better side won. Perhaps Liverpool's extra experience of the big occasion told in the end. You can never tell how Wembley tension is going to hit you until you get out there on the pitch. Our youngsters will know all about it next time. It's disappointing to finish second in both cup and League, but we have had a wonderful first season back in the First Division and I am very pleased with the team.'

It was a heavy week before the final because we played two games before heading off to London to prepare. We allowed ourselves to be caught up in the hullabaloo of a cup final and the younger players especially did find it, as for the match, difficult to relax.

Wembley has always been a bit of a jinx ground for me and it proved the case again. No excuses, the better team won; simple as that. The defence was superb, but Albert froze, Jim Storrie was injured, which made it hard for the midfield. That said,

Bobby and Don Revie share a joke with HRH Prince Philip.

Good luck!

I just didn't get into the game and had one of my worst games all season. Having said that, Billy scored a fantastic goal and I wish we'd have survived because we'd have had it over them in a replay. We could not have played as badly a second time.

When you get beaten in a final it's very hard to come up with words that can soothe anybody. Yes we had a nice banquet, but it would have been far better if we had won. The civic reception in Leeds was great; thousands turned out to welcome us back, which made us all the more determined. Coming so close to the double was a fantastic achievement because the club had never come close before. The buzz in the city was just amazing.

Looking back, one of the key reasons for our success was team spirit; it embraces everyone and was a major factor that season. Getting to the cup final was the highlight because you can never beat a first and Billy's goal meant that Leeds had reached an FA Cup final for the first time. It is a tournament that carries so much emotion and history, it was a magical moment.

149

They shall not pass…

Following the final the players received a tumultuous reception from supporters on their return to Leeds. Thousands welcomed them into Leeds city station and 60,000 thronged the route through Boar Lane, Briggate and the Headrow to the Civic Hall. The short trip, which took nearly one hour was headed by mounted police and the Leeds pipe band. At the Civic Hall the Lord Mayor, Alderman Mrs Lizzie Naylor welcomed Don Revie, Harry Reynolds, Bobby Collins and his teammates prior to speeches and a reception in the Banqueting Hall.

The Lord Mayor: 'We welcome our great football team back from Wembley and congratulate them on their achievements this season. I think this is the most exciting day of my life. We are not downhearted because we will win the cup. Many opportunities lie ahead. They have put themselves on the football map and brought lustre to this city. This is not the end, only the beginning.'

Don Revie: 'To be a big club we have to take setbacks and carry on. If we can't take defeat we will never be a club. If you give support like this year's we will give everything in our power to pay you back.'

Bobby Collins stepped forward: 'We were just beaten for the League and unfortunately we got beaten yesterday. There are a lot of people who underrated us and now, I think, there are a lot of them who admire us. Next year I am quite sure the boys will make a great effort to bring the Cup back.'

Harry Reynolds: 'I am sure they deserve every bit of praise you have given them. Although we have made much progress this year this is only the start. We all hope we will be back at Wembley next year and we will also win the League Championship. I am proud to think I am connected with Leeds United. For years we have struggled. Now we have achieved a little success but we can do better. Our aim is to top not only the English but European football.'

Lord Harewood: 'What you have won is renown, and that is something Leeds United did not possess before. We have had great players at Elland Road before, like Edwards, Copping and John Charles, but this is without any shadow of doubt the best team we have ever had. I don't think any supporter thinks differently. To have gathered 61 points in a season yet still fail to get the Football League Championship is unique in football records.'

Looking back on a memorable season, Phil Brown of the *Green Post* noted: 'Nobody who has followed Leeds United this season should be short of memories. There has been an almost meteor-like quality in United's reappearance on the top deck of football. They have sped through the First Division and through the Cup in turn to the twin heights straight from the comparative obscurity of the Second Division. But meteor-like is perhaps not the best term, for meteors burn our. There will be no sudden burning out at Elland Road.'

United chairman Mr Harry Reynolds told Brown: 'We have had two successful years at Elland Road, re-establishing the club and the team. They have been hard

Bobby and Jack Charlton look on as Gary Sprake catches cleanly.

Left: Get in there!

Below: The dream is over.

Returning heroes.

and tiring years, but the real hard work is only starting. There can be no standing still in top-class soccer just as there can be no standing still in top-class business or industry. United must go on building, strengthening and seeking new ideas. Our most dangerous opponents will be doing the same. We must be in there with them, preferably ahead of them. The last thing we intend to do at Elland Road is to ease up now that momentum has been gained, our crowd has come back bigger than ever, the club is better organised than ever, and the team is playing better than ever.'

Before the season some pundits were predicting that we would go down because we were too inexperienced at this level. At the start teams did underestimate us, but we were in really good shape and if we went a goal up it was very rare that we lost.

We were vying with Manchester United for the title right to the end. Losing on goal average was difficult to take. Maybe it would have been better if there was a play-off, but we'd done incredibly well. In the end we finished runners-up in both League and FA Cup. It was disappointing of course, but what a season. Our supporters had never seen anything like it and of course it heralded the future for the club. We had broken through.

I was delighted for Don. He was the reason why I joined Leeds. Don could size up someone quickly and I knew we could work together. Making his point precisely he

153

Thanks for your support.

was not keen on flannel merchants. If Don felt that you could do a job for him, he would back you all the way. Being professional in outlook was everything to him. Don wanted first-class footballers and first-class citizens. His responsibility to the players did not end on the training ground or football pitch. Don always said that each apprentice had different characteristics so the club had to find a way to help them because it would help them succeed at the club.

Don set the highest standards in terms of effort and discipline because nothing could be achieved without total commitment. Everyone counted to him. The players, laundry and tea ladies, programmer sellers, everybody had something to contribute for the good of the club. Everyone thought I was crazy when I decided to go to Leeds, but it was the best thing I did in my career. Don built a team spirit that was second to none. There was a fierce loyalty to him, the club and the crowd. Now we were poised to win major competitions and play in Europe. Life could not have been better.

THIRTEEN

INDIAN SUMMER
1964-1965

On the international front, pundits had throughout the season been predicting Bobby Collins' return to the national side. Don Revie wrote in the *Weekly News*: 'I've never known a player like Bobby. He's a wonderful example to every player in the club, both on the field during a game and off the field after a game. He still goes all out for ninety minutes. When it comes to training, I have never come across anyone who trained harder or set a better example in enthusiasm. I don't know why Everton came to let him go, but I do know he's repaid his transfer several times over; in all he's had 115 games and only 21 losses. What's more, he's never played better than he's playing now. I don't know how your selectors can leave him out of the Scottish team. He's a natural to fill the place left by the late John White. What a forward line you (Scotland) could have at Wembley...Henderson, Collins, Gilzean, Law and Wilson.'

Back in the international fold.

Class of '65 (© *Scottish Daily Express*).

Bobby told reporters as speculation mounted:

I can't say I worry about caps, I think it's largely a matter of luck whether you're watched or not. It was back in 1959 when I last played for Scotland. That was on a Continental tour. We went to Denmark, Holland and Portugal and I played against the last two. Frankly, I think I play exactly the same style of game today as I did then. I'm still an all-action type. I'm still scoring goals and making them. I'm still 5ft 3in and 9st 12lb. I don't think I'm a veteran, in fact, I can honestly say I'm enjoying my football now better than I ever did.

Leeds is a wonderful club to be with. There's a great atmosphere all the way through. Players, manager, directors, you feel you all 'belong'. I couldn't be happier. I'm not even thinking about retiring as a player, but when I do, I'm hoping some club will be willing to take me as a manager. Football means that much to me.

Following Leeds' win over Manchester United in the FA Cup semi-finals, Bobby earned a recall to the full Scottish side to face England at Wembley. He was delighted to be playing in such exalted company as Jimmy Johnstone, Charlie Cook, Denis Law and Jim Baxter.

With the side in the middle of World Cup qualifiers against Finland, Poland and Italy it was a remarkable comeback. Ken Gallagher commented in the *Daily Record*: 'The

Ready for anything... Henderson, Collins, Law, Wilson and St John.

Peter Pan of English football, little Bobby Collins of Leeds United, yesterday completed a Wembley double he never believed he could reach, the international against England and the English cup final. The Collins-Charlton partnership has brought Leeds a load of goals this year. A year that has capped a tremendous comeback for the man they call the Little Lord Mayor of Leeds, the little man who was so nearly forgotten just three seasons ago. But with a heart as big as himself, Collins was bounded back to greatness and how sorry Everton must be that they sold this inside-forward genius to Leeds. In his three seasons with the Yorkshire club, Collins has carried them from the bottom of the Second Division to promotion and the now to Wembley. I'm certain that Collins and Denis Law will be as exciting and as profitable a partnership as John White and Law were before.'

FOOTBALL ASSOCIATION INTERNATIONAL

SATURDAY APRIL 10th 1965 · Kick·off 3 p.m.

ENGLAND
v
SCOTLAND

Official Programme   One Shilling

EMPIRE
STADIUM

What a comeback… a clash against the Auld Enemy!

Bobby told Gallagher:

These have been the greatest twenty-four hours in my life. I didn't believe it possible for me to get back into Scotland's team. Now here it is for real. I'll be playing my heart out at Wembley. It's wonderful to find your way back into a Scottish jersey. After all, I thought my career as far as internationals went, was finished. It's been a fantastic season; probably the best in my life and this is a tremendous climax. I'd like nothing better than to help beat England again and then go on and play in the World Cup, but it's going to be funny placing crosses into goal against Jackie Charlton instead of for him.

Ken Jones in the *Daily Mirror* singled Collins out as the key threat to England: 'No heart will glow with fiercer pride at Wembley today than the one that drives the sixty-three-inch frame of Bobby Collins. England must match that heart beat for beat if they are to succeed or even survive against Scotland in a match that matters so much to so many. Collins, the "Little Caesar" of Leeds, commando captain of the season's shock side, comes back to international football with six years separating him from his previous cap. He comes back in form, on top, typifying the spirit of Scotland with every fierce demanding challenge for the ball. A challenge that shames every man who has ever shirked a tackle. Collins for me is the key to it all. His tiny feet hit the ball with great length and accuracy. His footballing vision is so sharp that he seems to see everything at the right time. His competitive approach is so fierce that it is virtually impossible to detail one man to mark him out of the game, and even in the evening of his career he seems to have found the sort of stamina that not even the holding Wembley turf can kill. If allowed, Collins can cut great holes in England's defence.'

On the day, in a battling display, Scotland fought back from two goals behind to draw 2-2. The match saw the full debut of Bobby's Leeds teammate Billy Bremner, brought in as a late reserve, but it was Law and St John who made the headlines with goals, although Bobby played his part. Bobby recalls:

It was terrific to suddenly be recalled to the Scottish side by manager Ian McColl. It began something of an 'Indian Summer' for me and gave me the opportunity to line up with some fantastic players. We had some side and really when I think back we should have been more successful than we were. I was at the veteran stage but there was so much talent in that side. The trouble we had was striking the balance to playing as a team as opposed to individuals. We performed well against England and were a shade unfortunate not to pinch a win because it was a great fightback.

At the end of the season, Bobby faced Spain at Hampden, before leaving on a post-season tour to Poland and Finland for World Cup qualification matches.

This was one of the roughest internationals that I ever experienced. We drew 0-0 and in the aftermath the manager was dismissed. With World Cup qualification clashes with Poland and Italy coming up I wondered whether it would also signal an end to

Bobby battles for possession in a World Cup clash with Spain.

my international playing days, but I needn't have worried as my old teammate Jock Stein was appointed.

I'd played with him and had seen him coach, now I would experience his management style and I was not disappointed. Jock 'filled' a room with his personality. When he walked in he took over, everyone listened. We only had a brief time to prepare but he instantly gained everyone's confidence.

Previously we had played on away trips defensively with attack a possibility, Jock's style of play was more one of attack with defence in mind. I played a link role in his 4-2-4 system, which suited me fine.

In front of a capacity crowd in Poland, in torrential rain, Scotland drew 1-1, Denis Law equalising fourteen minutes from time after Lentner had given the Poles a second-half lead.

It was another hard match, and we did well, but I was rested for the Finland match. I was ready for a rest but it had been quite a season.

FOURTEEN

TORINO TRAGEDY
1965-1967

The 1965/66 campaign should have been one of the most memorable in Bobby Collins' career. After all, he was the reigning Footballer of the Year, skipper of the most improved side in England, a member of Scotland's international squad and playing in Europe for the first time at club level. Tragically, Bobby's season was destroyed following an horrendous injury in Italy.

The League campaign had begun brightly for Leeds. Six victories, including hard-earned wins against Sunderland, Nottingham Forest and Spurs, in the opening 10 matches saw them riding high in the League. In addition Revie's team were holding a slender advantage in their first ever Fairs Cup tie. Tragically though, having won a tricky fixture against Torino 2-1, heartbreak would strike in the return leg as Collins and co. battled towards a 0-0 draw.

We had been hanging on to our aggregate lead when Italian full-back Poletti scythed me down with a terrible challenge. The pain was agonising and I knew immediately that my leg was badly broken. Les Cocker came on and supervised as I was carried off to be taken to hospital. Willie Bell, who had been in the squad but was watching in the stadium, escorted me and helped keep the stretcher and my leg steady. The only fortunate thing, though I didn't realise it at the time, was that I was seen at a local hospital that specialised in repairing shattered limbs. Surrounded by mountains they had gained a reputation in this field having dealt with many ski and mountaineering casualties. They had perfected techniques for all kinds of fractures. The medical team was headed by a world renowned surgeon, Professor Re. I could not have been in better hands. The Professor assessed the injury and operated immediately. When I came round he told me that he had reset my shattered thigh bone with a fifteen-inch pin and was confident that I would play again with the pin inside, which was very reassuring. Leeds flew Beryl and Robert out to be with me, and throughout my two-week stay at the hospital I had plenty of visitors, including the entire Torino side. Poletti was particularly apologetic, but it didn't stop him injuring another player in the next match! The flight home wasn't the most comfortable as I had a special cast devised only for reclining seats, but they didn't recline. Back home I immediately began my rehabilitation under Les and Doc Adams. The pin was hollow, which enabled it to stay in my leg as I regained fitness. It stayed there for two years, before Mr Archie McDougall, an orthopaedic surgeon in Glasgow, removed it. The injury effectively ended my career at Leeds.

Don Revie commented in the *Daily Express*: 'We would rather have lost this game, not even been in the competition, if we had known that this would happen. I look upon Bobby as a teacher on the field. His enthusiasm, know-how and ability has rubbed off on the youngsters and is all around the club. Leeds United will never ever be able to repay him.'

Bobby's misfortune signalled the emergence of Johnny Giles, who recalled the poignancy in *The Leeds United Story*: 'It was the turning point of my career. I have always been a bit embarrassed by the fact that I benefited though Bobby's misfortune; like everyone else at Elland Road I had enormous respect for him. As a captain, Bobby was fantastic. He knew the right psychological moment for lifting you up or for giving you a deserved rollicking, and he helped me more than I can say. When I joined Leeds,

Leeds United, 1965/66. *From left to right, back row:* Bell, Reaney, Lorimer, Belfitt, Cooper. Middle row: Collins, Hunter, Williamson, Sprake, Greenhoff, Madeley. *Front row:* Johnson, Storrie, Charlton, Peacock, Bremner, Giles, Johanneson.

Tee-off time!

my game lacked 'devil', and it was due mainly to Bobby's influence that I improved this aspect of my game.'

The injury cost Bobby his Leeds United and Scottish place. By the end of his international career only Denis Law and Jimmy McMeneny had enjoyed longer Scotland careers than Bobby Collins. During his fifteen-year association with the national side he had converted from an inside forward to a key central midfielder. Tenacious in attack and defence during the late 1950's, nobody scored more goals than he did.

It was a terrible way to end to my international career, but looking back I could have few complaints. I'd enjoyed the challenge of international football and pitting my wits against the world's best. Playing international football you soon got used to European sides' time-wasting tactics. It could be frustrating, but you had to be patient and wait for your opportunities. Opposing players would try their best to intimidate you at every opportunity and it was important to keep your head and not lose your temper. I'd played against all the greats of my era, players such as Alfredo di Stefano, Ferenc Puskas, Duncan Edwards, Billy Wright, Bert Trautmann and Bobby Charlton.

Larking about... Billy Bremner, Big Jack and the skipper.

European bow.

I'd also scored at the World Cup, which only a few Scots can boast. That was all in the past for me though as the battle was on to get fit for domestic football. Not many people gave me a chance but I was determined.

As Bobby began the long road back to fitness he talked about Leeds United's rise under Don Revie in the *Charles Buchan Soccer Gift Book*, 1965/66. The article was titled *What A Difference Success Makes!*

A team is only as good as its last match. A club is as good as its last season's record. No matter how bright the prospect seems, what you have done is the yardstick and by that judgement, Leeds United are a very good team, a big club. We are rightly proud of our achievements and will remember forever the intense support we have had from the city.
I signed for United on 8 March 1962. It had hurt me to learn that Everton felt they could afford to let me go so I determined to show that wee Bobby Collins still had a lot to offer. It's hard now to picture the miserable 9,000 fans spread round the Elland Road ground when I came in against Swansea Town. Only Jack Charlton, Willie Bell, Billy Bremner and Albert Johanneson are still in our side with me. Fellows like Tommy Younger, Greenville Hair, Freddie Goodwin, Cliff Mason and Eric Smith have

moved on. To them, and other, must go the credit for saving us from the drop. Their great effort swung the club from danger and gave us the chance to build up to what we have now. In our desperate year we won 4, drew 6 and lost 1 of our last 11 games; 14 points from a possible 22. Not record-breaking stuff but good enough to keep us up.

So much has changed since then. In those early, dark days, I could walk through the town and few knew me or wanted to. Now it's not easy to walk anywhere without being caught up in football talk! Don Revie is behind the revival; he and a board of directors who have backed him all the way. Revie pitched in youngsters like Gary Sprake, Paul Reaney and Norman Hunter. I felt some responsibility towards these youngsters. I found myself watching them closely, advising, coaxing and sometimes bullying, to bring them into the pattern of the team. They grew up rapidly indeed! Team spirit is the key to United's rise in the game. No club has a bigger stock of the commodity in its dressing rooms.

By the end of the season, just as he had forecast, Bobby was back in the first team. Playing in the last match, a 1-1 draw at Manchester United courtesy of a rare Paul

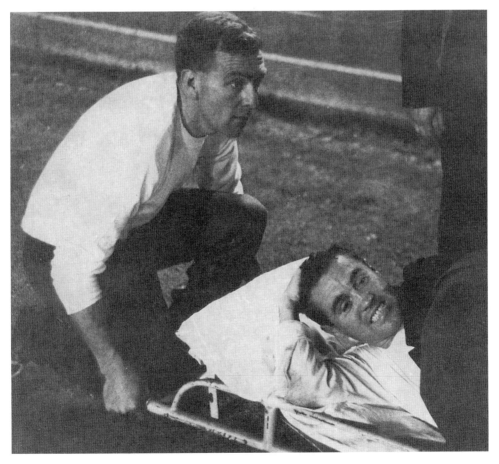

Agony in Torino.

Reaney goal, Leeds finished runners-up for the second successive season; this time behind Liverpool. It was an amazing comeback.

It was great to be back and prove all the doubters wrong. I was determined to get even stronger for the start of new campaign.

At the beginning of the 1966/67 campaign, Bobby lined up for the opening game of the season at Tottenham Hotspur. Leeds lost 3-1, but reporters were only interested in one player. Peter Lorenzo wrote in the *Sun*: 'By rights Bobby Collins should have been one of the spectators at Tottenham, but on a day when most came to applaud the £585,019 skills of Spurs, they were caught in mid-cheer and left to marvel at the stamina, snappy

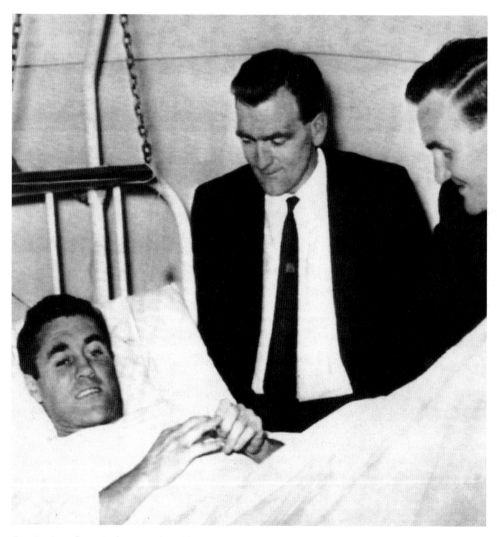

Don Revie and Les Cocker console Bobby as he begins the long road back.

Fighting fit!

aggression and superb skills of Collins. What an amazing man! What a courageous example for any footballer, at any level! In a game that should have been dominated by England, Venables and their high-priced buddies, the Man-of-the-Match accolade was won hands down by a pocket-sized dynamo, a player small in everything but heart and ability.'

This was the game when Billy upset Dave Mackay with a challenge and Dave grabbed Billy by the scruff of the neck and nearly lifted him off the floor. Billy could get opponents riled.

Bobby played his part in Leeds' opening home win against West Brom, but would not be back in the side until a trip to Hillsborough as Christmas approached. Donning the number ten shirt for a four-match run, Bobby helped Leeds remain unbeaten against Sheffield Wednesday, Blackpool, Tottenham and Newcastle United. Following an emotional return to European action against Valencia, there would be one final appearance against Stoke City at Elland Road for supporters to marvel at the maestro before Bobby Collins accepted the inevitable and joined Second Division strugglers Bury on a free transfer in February 1967. His influence at Leeds United will never be forgotten.

Don Revie in *The Leeds United Story* said: 'He is the perfect example of what we in the game call a professional's professional. Bobby's aim was always to do things simply and quickly. He never tried to be too clever on the ball for the sake of his own glory.

'I have never come across anyone with such a fierce will-to-win and dedication to the game. These qualities immediately rubbed off on the players around him at Elland Road, from the juniors to the first teamer's. Bobby regarded it as a personal insult to be beaten. I had been searching for some time for a midfield 'general' with the character and skill to really motivate the team, and Bobby fitted the bill perfectly.'

Billy Bremner said of Bobby in *The Legend of Billy Bremner*: 'Bobby Collins was the best professional I have ever known. He was thirty-one when he joined us and everyone else was writing him off, but he stayed for several years and he played at the top of his game throughout. Even when he was seriously injured he came bouncing back to lead us to new heights. All the young players who were around at the time owed Bobby Collins a big debt for his generalship, his advice and his example.

'Whenever he was in the side I felt confident that he would bully, coax, cajole, cool us down when we were in danger of losing our heads, encourage and praise us whenever we did anything good, and generally looked after us like a father. In the heat of the game he would sense when we were beginning to need a bit of breathing space, and then he would go into the fight for possession of the ball, and plonk a pass up the wing for Albert Johanneson to chase, while we at the back breathed a little less hard, and pulled ourselves together.

'When Bobby went out to play, nothing could put him off his game. He left his cares behind him in the dressing room, and for the next ninety minutes only one thing mattered, that everyone should be pulling his guts out for the whole ninety minutes, in a tremendous team effort.

Merry Christmas… but Bobby's days
at Leeds are numbered.

'I learned many great lessons from Bobby Collins, not the least being able to take the knocks as well as hand them out and always play the game as a man. They say that one man doesn't make a team – but Bobby Collins came nearer to doing it than anyone else I have ever seen on a football field.'

Johnny Giles: 'I arrived at Leeds from Manchester United a couple of games into the 1963/64 season and I immediately got a sense of team spirit and this great drive to do well, which Bobby was leading at the club. We had a great season, losing just 3 matches in 42, which was unbelievable and was a key reason why we won the Championship. Yet funnily enough we lost against the leading teams, Sunderland and Preston, so had a lot to do and get ahead of them.

'Promotion was a huge target for the club, because we weren't well-fancied like Sunderland and Preston but they didn't have the drive that we had to win matches, and to do it on a consistent level. Strangely, our away record was very good in comparison to our home form where we drew a lot of matches against teams that we should have been beating, but having the players we had in those days suited us better away from home. We clinched promotion at Swansea, where we won comfortably, and at Charlton we clinched the title with a fine win.

We were underestimated at the start of the 1964/65 season because we were not a fashionable team. We had just been promoted, had a lot of young players in the side, but the team had a particular drive to do well and work hard. It stemmed from Don, but you also had to have someone on the pitch, and we had Bobby Collins. Bobby had this incredible drive himself and there is nothing better than having someone on the pitch that is setting an example. The message was clear; this was the standard needed and Bobby was doing it week after week. What Leeds did during the season was remarkable. We took Liverpool, who were a great side and the defending Champions; to extra-time in the cup final and it was the first time that a team had gained 60 points but did not win the League. The campaign was one of the great achievements by Leeds United.

'Bobby's impact on Leeds United was immeasurable. He was older than the rest of the players and set the standards of how a top professional should look after himself. Bobby's attitude was great and his will to win was unbelievable. Bobby thought he could and should win every match he played in, and that rubbed off on the rest of the players. Of course his attitude to winning was mainly effective on the pitch because we saw how he prepared right and drove himself on. Long after Bobby had left, his influence stayed with the players.'

I'd signed a new contract before I got injured but it was time to move on. Johnny Giles and Billy Bremner had teamed up in midfield and you could see they would be superb together. When I arrived at Leeds United, thoughts of championships, cup finals and European finals were just dreams. By my departure they had started to become a reality, which was extremely rewarding. I'm glad I was at Leeds at the start of their revival and was able to help build a side that would become respected throughout Europe.

FIFTEEN

GLOBETROTTER
1967-1971

Life after Leeds was a rollercoaster during Bobby's two-year stint at Bury. Shortly after signing for the Second Division outfit, he told Gerry Loftus of the *Sunday Citizen*:

Whether I'll be able to do enough to help them clear of trouble it's far too early to say, but I will be doing everything possible. The Bury lads are keen, so all of us will be

New challenge… Bury, 1967. *From left to right, back row:* Les Hart (Physiotherapist), J. Wheeler, Brian Turner, Roy Parnell, Hugh Tinney, Ray Parry, Neil Ramsbottom, George Jones, Alex Lindsay, Jimmy Kerr, Les Shannon (Manager). *Front row:* Greg Farrell, Tommy Claxton, Alex Dawson, Bobby Collins (Capt.) Roy Hughes, Bobby Owen. Absent, Brian Grundy.

In action for Bury (© UPPA).

having a real try. In my first couple of games the opposition put a man to mark me and this is something for which you cannot plan a rigid counter. The Bury team hasn't been together very long and it will take time for understanding to be reached so that we can make full use of the situations that arise.

Manager Les Shannon said: 'He is the ideal player to get the side on its feet. We have a lot of very useful young players but through lack of experience, they are inclined to panic. Bobby can provide the steadying influence we have lacked and, if he can do for us just a fraction of what he did for Leeds, we will be very happy.'

Unfortunately, Bobby was too late to help his new team avoid relegation alongside Northampton Town, but he did help his new charges bounce back the following season as runners-up in the Third Division. It was mighty close though; 2 points separated Champions Oxford United from third-placed Shrewsbury Town, and 7 points split the top eight.

Bury's 24 wins were actually the highest in the League, but 14 defeats meant they finished the 1967/68 campaign 1 point adrift of Oxford with 55 points from their 46 games. Missing just 3 games, Bobby had been a central figure in the success, but Bury were unable to maintain their League status the following term. Finishing with 33 points, they slipped back to the Third Division along with Fulham. By the final games however, when relegation was sealed, Bobby had moved on to pastures new with Scottish First Division side Morton. Signed in April 1969 for his experience, Bobby was charged with helping youngsters such as Joe Jordan settle in first team football. At the time Morton had just been knocked out of the Scottish Cup at the semi-final stage by Celtic, who went on to lift the trophy, following a 4-0 over Rangers. Making his debut at the start of the 1969/70 campaign against St Mirren in the League Cup, following a 1-0 win, Bobby told David Allister of the *Scottish Daily Express*:

That was really hectic out there. Is every match as helter-skelter? I couldn't get a breather. Down south they play it across the park until an opening shows and then it's all go for goal. Out there it was the through ball all the time with everyone chasing it like mad. I'm a bit behind the others in training and games but I'll catch up fast. I'll have to if that pace is the general yardstick!

During Bobby's spell at the club, Morton enjoyed one of the best periods in the club's history. It also gave the Wee Barra the opportunity to return to his former club.

Going back to Celtic was fantastic; it was as if I'd never been away and I was delighted to see Jock Stein again. Jimmy Gribben was also still at the club; Jock had not forgotten how he'd helped him out all those years ago. I felt at home, though incredibly it had been twenty-one years since I'd signed as a player for Celtic.

Bobby returns to his Scottish roots.

Welcome home!

Morton finished comfortably in the top ten during his two-year spell, and for the veteran player it had been a success. Looking back one game stood out; the day little Morton defeated mighty Rangers 2-0 at Ibrox. A member of the Morton team that day was young teenage striker Jordan, just making his way in the game. Joe would go on to score in three World Cups for Scotland and become a legend at Leeds United, Manchester United and AC Milan: 'I followed Celtic as a youngster so was well aware of Bobby's achievements as a player. I'd never seen Bobby play but I'd read about his career. He was held in high esteem by everyone because he'd made his mark in Scottish football history. When he arrived at Morton, Bobby was the elder statesman of the team and it was a privilege to play with him. I only made a few appearances before I joined Leeds United, but one game I recall was when we won at Rangers. It was a great win for us and Bobby scored one of our goals.'

I grabbed a goal, which was really pleasing. I remember playing a ball wide and running through for the return. After sidestepping the goalkeeper, I stopped the ball on the line and waited for the defender to come back. As he approached, I waited until the last moment before crashing it into the roof of the net. The look on home supporter's faces was priceless!

Just before beginning a new chapter in his career, Morton played a Leeds United XI at Cappielow Park as a curtain-raiser to the 1971/72 campaign. The match, prematurely as future events transpired, was billed as his last in Britain. Don Revie refused to play a weakened side, as a tribute to his former skipper, and Leeds ran out comfortable 4-1 winners.

A local paper reported: 'Bobby Collins ended his remarkable twenty-two-year career in British football amid emotional scenes. Before the kick off, both teams formed an avenue to applaud the forty-year-old midfield veteran on to the pitch. Leeds United captain Johnny Giles and Morton chairman Peter Scott made presentations to Collins on behalf of both clubs.'

As the two teams began their respective campaigns, Bobby Collins flew off to Australia where he joined Ringwood City on 12 August 1971. Sadly, the move didn't work out despite him transforming the club within two months. *The Sporting Globe* reported: 'Bobby Collins, the King of Victorian Soccer, has abdicated. There were some sad faces at Ringwood during the week when he said goodbye to his teammates. In the short time he had been with them, he became one of the most popular players in the club. There is no doubt that he made a big impact on the club from the day he arrived. Bobby, forty, is the greatest player to kick the round-ball in Victorian League

Goal! Bobby grabs the winner against Rangers (© *The Scottish Daily Record*).

Final game...maybe not.

competition. He acted as 'field marshal' when playing against opposing teams. Many games were won by Ringwood with him directing play on the field and giving teammates the great benefit of his professional experience. Nothing was too much for him. It is hard to believe that one man could do so much for a team who earlier in the season looked like being relegated to the Metropolitan League. With Bobby's appearance the club finished in fifth place.'

In October 1971, as Bobby prepared to fly home, an opportunity materialised in Hong Kong, but he quickly turned it down in favour of an offer to coach top Sydney club Hakoah Eastern Suburbs. Unfortunately this post would last only ten months.

There were numerous reasons that undermined my ability to coach the team; the worst being continual interference from people within the club on team selection. I left the team at the top of the table, so it was difficult to believe I'd failed.

Bobby flew back to Leeds and married his partner, Betty, on 28 July 1972 and returned to his former club to keep his fitness.

I played in a few practice games. Some of the Leeds lads were so impressed that I started thinking about playing again. I knew that I could coach, I wanted to be a manager eventually but there was no thrill quite like playing.

After playing a few games with Shamrock Rovers, an opportunity surfaced at Oldham Athletic. Bobby's arrival as player-coach at Oldham Athletic in October 1972 made headline news. With only a solitary victory in their opening 6 games Oldham were near the foot of the table. Bobby was cleared to play League football at the age of forty-one; however his main task would be to share responsibility for coaching the first XI with manager Jimmy Frizzell, Walter Joyce paying attention to the club's junior players. His influence was immediate as Oldham defeated Bristol Rovers, Rotherham, Plymouth and Blackburn. The only blot was a home defeat by Grimsby Town. After a win at Southend, Bobby returned to League action for a home clash against Wrexham. Following a 2-2 draw the media eulogised about the Peter Pan of football.

Frank Clough in the *Sun*: 'The Jimmy Cagney of British soccer is back…strutting, cussing, bawling, playing and loving every minute of it. Bobby Collins is the name, forty-one now and greying with it but still the same forceful, dynamic little character who became one of the games legends in the '60s. People who remember what a tough little nut he was at his peak, like me, wonder whether Collins might now become like the central figure in the classic Western situation, the retired gunfighter who comes back, a sitting target for a young tearaway to get a quick reputation by gunning him down.'

The veteran told Clough:

I admit I have murdered a few in my time and I have been murdered a few times myself as well. Don't forget this is a man's game, but if any young kid fancies 'doing' me to get a name for himself, I will give him a word of advice… don't give it unless you can take it and unless you know what you're doing. You can't say you haven't been warned lad! I'd like to play up to the end of the season and then see how I feel and see what turns up. I might carry on playing. I may turn to coaching; I might even try my hand at management somewhere. One thing is for sure, I'm not ready for that pine box yet.

Regarding the game Bobby said:

I dropped the clanger that produced their goal. I had an 'assist' in one of ours, and I got booked. Nothing's changed. I wondered how I was going to find it, but it wasn't hard at all. In fact, I was quite pleased with my running and my general mobility, although to be honest I gave the ball away a bit more often than I used to do. Lack of match practice I suppose.

Bobby played the next five games, yielding home wins against Scunthorpe United 3-0, Swansea City 2-0 and Plymouth Argyle 7-1. Following a heavy defeat at Grimsby, Bobby faced Scarborough in the first round of the FA Cup but there would be no cup joy although Bobby did score in a 2-1 defeat; his last strike in the professional game. By

The boss at Huddersfield (© West Riding News Service).

January 1973 Bobby was promoted to assistant manager and helped the team to fourth spot; playing his final ever match when he came on as a substitute against Rochdale during the run-in.

I had no complaints about hanging up my boots; after all I made my Celtic debut in 1949, so I'd had a fine run as a professional footballer.

Oldham began the new term in fine style, losing just once in the opening 17 matches. A blip followed at the turn of the year with 4 consecutive defeats, but 10 successive wins put them back on track for the title. Promotion was sealed with a 6-0 win at home to Huddersfield Town with 4 games to go. Two draws in remaining games sealed the title.

It was a very satisfying season for everyone and we deserved the title. Leeds won the Championship again that season and some years later I discovered that the players' mementos for both divisions were identical, apart from the inscription!

The success marked Bobby down as a potential manager, and it surprised few in the game when Third Division Huddersfield Town offered him his first managerial post as a replacement for Ian Greaves. His appointment was ratified during the World Cup finals. Having worked under Jimmy McGrory, Johnny Carey, Harry Catterick, Don Revie, Les Shannon and Jimmy Frizzell, Bobby had plenty of experience to draw upon. Confident of making an immediate impact, Bobby utilised thirty-three players but his debut season was a disaster. After losing 6 of their opening 8 games, Huddersfield steadied things briefly with a 6-match unbeaten run. Thereafter it would not be until March 1975 that the team recorded 2 consecutive wins, after which there would be just a sole victory in the last dozen games. Finishing bottom, Huddersfield had slumped into the bottom rung of the Football League for the first time in their proud history; a situation unimaginable when they won the Second Division title in 1969/70.

Determined to bounce back at the first attempt, directors hired Tom Johnston as general manager to work alongside Bobby for the new campaign. On 11 December 1975, Betty and Bobby celebrated the birth of their first child, Michael, but within days he was looking for another job after being dismissed on Christmas Eve. By July 1976 Bobby was back in employment at Leeds United as youth team coach. His tenure would

Bobby's boys… Leeds United youth team, 1976.

last twelve months before Hull City boss John Kaye appointed him coach of the Second Division club. Before long Bobby was caretaker manager when Kaye departed, and the appointment was made permanent following a fine win over promotion favourites Tottenham Hotspur. Sadly, his time at the helm would be brief. Just 4 wins in four months brought an end to his tenure as he became the shortest-reigning manager in the club's history.

Although I was made boss, it was quickly apparent that there were a lot of problems both on and off the field. I brought in Syd Owen, but we were not given time to turn things around. Billy Bremner was winding down his career and scored a few goals, but there was little we could do.

Bobby spent the final months of the 1977/78 season coaching at Blackpool before his appointment as youth team coach at Barnsley by former Leeds legend Norman Hunter. Following spells as assistant and caretaker-manager, Bobby would take the helm at Oakwell in February 1984. His tenure, however, would only last fifteen months.

During my one season as manager we finished mid-table and reached the quarter-finals of the FA Cup, which was some achievement, but during the close season the chairman let me go. I was disappointed as we had done well under the circumstances, but I shouldn't have been surprised because the one sure thing about being a manager is that one day you'll be sacked.

In charge at Barnsley, 1984/85 (© Stan Plus StanTwo).

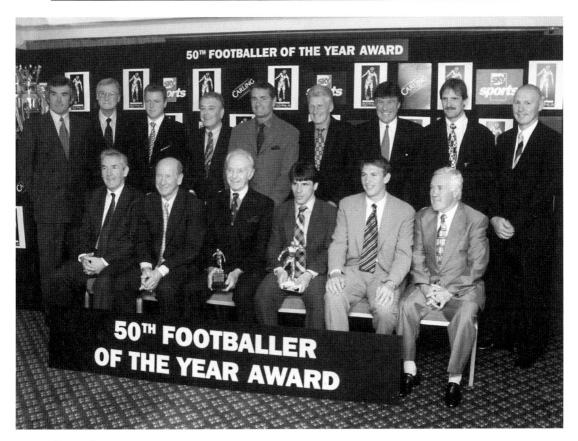

Star quality.

A regular member of Leeds United ex-players XI, Bobby ended his managerial career with a season in charge of Guisley Celtic in 1987/88. In April 1988 Leeds United awarded Bobby and John Charles a testimonial for their services to the club.

For many seasons Bobby has been a regular visitor at Elland Road and is welcomed by supporters as a legend. Now seventy-three, his efforts on behalf of the club will never be forgotten because Bobby Collins was Don Revie's most influential signing and he is one of the greatest players to ever represent Leeds United.

It takes a very special footballer to be regarded as a legend at clubs of the stature of Celtic, Everton and Leeds United. The 'Wee Barra' achieved this status with skill, professionalism and passion.

Right: Betty and Bobby 1995.

Below: Julie, Bobby, Betty and Michael at home, 2004.

CAREER STATISTICS

INTERNATIONAL CAREER

DOMESTIC CAREER:

GLASGOW CELTIC

EVERTON

LEEDS UNITED

BURY

GREENOCK MORTON

OLDHAM ATHLETIC

CUP FINAL APPEARANCES
& LEAGUE HONOURS

INTERNATIONAL CAREER

YEAR	DATE	VENUE	ATTENDANCE	OPPONENTS	RESULT	GOALS
1950	21-Oct	Cardiff	60,000	Wales	Won 3 - 1	
1950	01-Nov	Hampden Park	75,000	Northern Ireland	Won 6 - 1	
1950	13-Dec	Hampden Park	68,000	Austria	Lost 0 - 1	
1955	15-May	Belgrade	20,000	Yugoslavia	Drew 2 - 2	
1955	19-May	Vienna	65,000	Austria	Won 4 - 1	
1955	29-May	Budapest	102,000	Hungary	Lost 1 - 3	
1955	08-Oct	Belfast	50,000	Northern Ireland	Lost 1 - 2	
1955	09-Nov	Hampden Park	53,887	Wales	Won 2 - 0	
1956	20-Oct	Cardiff	60,000	Wales	Drew 2 - 2	
1957	06-Apr	Wembley	97,520	England	Lost 1 - 2	
1957	08-May	Hampden Park	89,000	Spain	Won 4 - 2	
1957	19-May	Basle	48,000	Switzerland	Won 2 - 1	One
1957	22-May	Stuttgart	80,000	West Germany	Won 3 - 1	Two
1957	26-May	Madrid	90,000	Spain	Lost 1 - 4	
1957	05-Oct	Belfast	58,000	Northern Ireland	Drew 1 - 1	
1957	06-Nov	Hampden Park	58,811	Switzerland	Won 3 - 2	
1957	13-Nov	Hampden Park	42,918	Wales	Drew 1 - 1	One
1958	07-May	Hampden Park	54,900	Hungary	Drew 1 - 1	

1958	01-Jun	Warsaw	70,000	Poland	Won 2 - 1	Two
1958	08-Jun	Vasteras	9,591	Yugoslavia *	Drew 1 - 1	
1958	11-Jun	Norrkoping	11,665	Paraguay *	Lost 2 - 3	One
1958	15-Jun	Orebro	13,554	France *	Lost 1 - 2	One
1958	18-Oct	Cardiff	60,000	Wales	Won 3 - 0	One
1958	05-Nov	Hampden Park	72,732	Northern Ireland	Drew 2 - 2	
1959	11-Apr	Wembley	98,329	England	Lost 0 - 1	
1959	06-May	Hampden Park	103,415	West Germany	Won 3 - 2	
1959	27-May	Amsterdam	55,000	Netherlands	Won 2 - 1	One
1959	03-Jun	Lisbon	30,000	Portugal	Lost 0 - 1	
1965	10-Apr	Wembley	98,199	England	Drew 2 - 2	
1965	08-May	Hampden Park	60,146	Spain	Drew 1 - 1	
1965	23-May	Chorzow	95,000	Poland	Drew 0 - 0	

* = IN WORLD CUP FINALS

Scottish League – 1951: Irish League & League of Ireland, 1952: Irish League & League of Ireland

1953: Football League, 1955: Football League, 1956: Irish League, Danish League, League of Ireland & Football League

1957: Irish League, League of Ireland & Football League

1958: Irish League, League of Ireland and Football League, 1959: Irish League

DOMESTIC CAREER

GLASGOW CELTIC

	League		Scottish Cup		League Cup		Glasgow Cup		Glasgow Charity Cup		All Comps.		Comments
	Apps.	Goals	Apps.	Goals	Apps.	Goals	Apps.	Goals	Apps.	Goals	Apps.	Goals	
1949 - 1950	26	7	4	0	6	1	1	0	1	0	38	8	Made debut vs. Rangers in the League Cup (won 3-2) on 13 Aug. 1949 in front of 71,000 spectators. Final league position was 5th. Won Glasgow Charity Cup.
1950 - 1951	27	15	7	2	8	3	4	0	1	0	47	20	Final league position was 7th. Won Scottish Cup. Glasgow Cup and Glasgow Charity Cup runners-up. Scored hat-trick vs. East Fife (League) on 16 Dec.
1951 - 1952	30	12	2	0	8	1	2	3	0	0	42	16	Final league position was 9th. Glasgow Cup runners-up. Scored hat-trick vs. Third Lanark (Glasgow Cup) on 3 Sept.
1952 - 1953	14	3	5	0	0	0	0	0	2	0	21	3	Final league position was 8th. Won Glasgow Charity Cup.
1953 - 1954	25	10	0	0	4	0	3	0	1	0	33	10	League Champions. Won Scottish Cup. Glasgow Charity Cup runners-up. Scored hat-trick (all penalties) vs. Aberdeen (League) on 26 Sept.
1954 - 1955	20	5	7	1	2	1	0	0	1	0	30	7	League runners-up. Scottish Cup runners-up.
1955 - 1956	25	4	4	4	6	3	4	2	0	0	40	13	Final league position was 5th. Scottish Cup runners-up. Won Glasgow Cup.
1956 - 1957	20	5	6	2	11	4	1	0	1	0	39	11	Final league position was 5th. Won Scottish League Cup.
1957 - 1958	30	19	3	1	10	7	1	0	2	0	46	27	Final league position was 3rd. Won Scottish League Cup. Scored hat-trick (1 penalty) vs. Airdrie (League) on 22 March.
1958 - 1959	2	1	0	0	7	6	1	0	0	0	10	7	Final league position was 6th. Won Glasgow Charity Cup (after leaving the club). Last game was on 10 Sept. 1958 vs. Cowdenbeath in the League Cup (won 2-0).
TOTALS	220	81	38	10	62	26	17	5	9	0	346	122	Equivalent of a goal every 2.84 games.

Also played in the St. Mungo Cup on 14, 19, 20, 28 July and 1 August 1951 (semi-final and final at Hampden Park) vs. Hearts (won 2-1), Clyde (draw 4-4 scoring two goals including one penalty), Clyde (won replay 4-1), Raith Rovers (won 3-1)and Aberdeen (won 3-2).

Also played in the Coronation Cup on 11, 16 and 20 May 1953 at Hampden Park vs. Arsenal (scored in a 1-0 win), Manchester United (won 2-1) and Hibernian (2-0 win in the final).

EVERTON

	League		F. A. Cup		League Cup		All Comps.		Comments
	Apps.	Goals	Apps.	Goals	Apps.	Goals	Apps.	Goals	
1958 - 1959	32	7	4	3			36	10	Made debut vs. Manchester City in the League (won 3-1 and scored) on 13 Sept. 1958. Final league position was 16th.
1959 - 1960	42	14	1	0			43	14	Final league position was 16th.
1960 - 1961	40	16	1	0	5	1	46	17	Final league position was 5th. Scored two hat-tricks vs. Newcastle United (League) and Cardiff City (League) on 19 Nov. and 15 April.
1961 - 1962	19	5	3	2	0	0	22	7	Final league position was 4th. Last game was on 3 Mar. 1962 vs. Wolves in the League (won 4-0).
TOTALS	133	42	9	5	5	1	147	48	Equivalent of a goal every 3.06 games.

LEEDS UNITED

	League		F. A. Cup		League Cup		Inter-Cities F. Cup		Glasgow Charity Cup		All Comps.		Comments
	Apps.	Goals	Apps.	Goals	Apps.	Goals	Apps.	Goals	Apps.	Goals	Apps.	Goals	
1961 - 1962	11	1	0	0	0	0	0	0	0	0	11	1	Made debut vs. Swansea Town in the League (won 2-0 and scored) on 10 Mar. 1962. Final league position in Division Two was 19th.
1962 - 1963	41	8	3	1	0	0	0	0	0	0	44	9	Final league position was 5th. in Division Two
1963 - 1964	41	6	2	0	1	0	0	0	0	0	44	6	League Division Two Champions.
1964 - 1965	39	9	8	0	1	1	0	0	0	0	48	10	League (Division One) runners-up. F. A. Cup runners-up. Was voted Footballer of the Year (aged 34).
1965 - 1966	10	0	0	0	0	0	2	0	0	0	12	0	League runners-up.
1966 - 1967	7	0	0	0	0	0	1	0	1	0	9	0	Inter-cities Fairs Cup runners-up. Last game was on 11 Feb. 1967 vs. Stoke City in the League (won 3-0). Final league position was 4th.
TOTALS	149	24	13	1	2	1	3	0	1	0	168	26	Equivalent of a goal every 6.46 games.

Also played in the West Riding Cup on 7 May 1964 at Elland Road vs. Bradford City (scored two in a 4-1 win) and on May 20 1966 at Park Avenue vs. Bradford (won 4-0).

BURY

	League		F. A. Cup		League Cup		All Comps.		Comments
	Apps.	Goals	Apps.	Goals	Apps.	Goals	Apps.	Goals	
1966 - 1967	10	0	0	0	0	0	10	0	Made debut vs. Blackburn Rovers in the League Division Two (lost 1-2) on 25 Feb. 1967. Final league position in Division Two was 22nd. (bottom and relegated).
1967 - 1968	43	4	3	1	4	0	50	5	League Division Three runners-up.
1968 - 1969	22	2	1	0	1	0	24	2	Final league position in Division Two was 21st. (one from bottom and relegated). Last game was on 15 Apr. 1969 vs. Bristol City in Division Two (lost 1-2).
TOTALS	75	6	3	1	4	0	84	7	Equivalent of a goal every 12 games.

GREENOCK MORTON

	League		Scottish Cup		League Cup		Texaco Cup		All Comps.		Comments
	Apps.	Goals	Apps.	Goals	Apps.	Goals	Apps.	Goals	Apps.	Goals	
1969 - 1970	28	2	2	0	0	0	0	0	30	2	Made debut vs. St. Mirren in the League Cup (won 1-0) in Aug. 1969. Final league position in Division One was 9th.
1970 - 1971	27	1	1	0	0	0	4	0	32	1	Final league position in Division One was 8th. Last game was in May 1971 vs. St. Johnstone in the League (drew 0-0).
TOTALS	55	3	3	0	0	0	4	0	62	3	Equivalent of a goal every 20.67 games.

OLDHAM ATHLETIC

	League		F. A. Cup		League Cup		All Comps.		Comments
	Apps.	Goals	Apps.	Goals	Apps.	Goals	Apps.	Goals	
1972-1973	7	0	2	1	0	0	9	1	Made debut vs. Wrexham in the League (drew 2-2) on 14 Oct. 1972. Final league position in Division Three was 4th. Last game was on 20 Apr. 1973 (aged 42) vs. Rochdale in the League (drew 0-0).
TOTALS	7	0	2	1	0	0	9	1	Equivalent of a goal every 9 games.

TOTAL (ALL CLUBS)

	League		Scottish Cup / F. A. Cup		League Cup		GL./I.C.F./Tex Cups		Glasgow Charity Cup		All Comps.		Comments
	Apps.	Goals	Apps.	Goals	Apps.	Goals	Apps.	Goals	Apps.	Goals	Apps.	Goals	
1949-1973	639	156	68	18	73	28	24	5	10	0	814	207	Equivalent of a goal every 3.93 games.

Coaching / Managerial Career - Player-coach at Ringwood City, Melbourne, Australia in 1971, Player-coach at Hakoah, Sydney, Australia in 1971, (both of these positions were undertaken between his appearances for Greenock Morton and Oldham Athletic). Player-coach at Oldham Athletic in 1972 - 73 before being promoted to Assistant Manager in 1973 (Also played a few games for Shamrock Rovers whilst at Oldham Athletic). Manager at Huddersfield Town from 1974 - 75. Youth Coach at Leeds United in 1976. Coach at Hull City before being promoted to Manager in 1977 - 78. Coach at Blackpool in 1978. Youth Coach at Barnsley in 1980 before being promoted to Manager in 1984 - 85. Manager at Guisley in 1987.

CUP FINAL APPEARANCES & LEAGUE HONOURS

GLASGOW CELTIC – 1950 Glasgow Charity Cup - Winners, 1951 Scottish Cup - Winners, Glasgow Cup - Runners-up and Glasgow Charity Cup - Runners-up, 1952 Glasgow Cup - Runners-up, 1953 Glasgow Charity Cup - Winners, 1954 League Champions and Glasgow Charity Cup - Runners-up, 1955 League Runners-up and Scottish Cup Runners-up (played in drawn first final), 1956 Glasgow Cup - Winners, 1957 Scottish League Cup - Winners and 1958 Scottish League Cup - Winners.

LEEDS UNITED – 1964 Division Two Champions, 1965 Division One Runners-up and F. A. Cup Runners-up and 1966 Division One Runners-up.

BURY – 1968 Division Three Runners-up.

If you are interested in purchasing
other books published by Tempus, or in case you have
difficulty finding any Tempus books in your local bookshop,
you can also place orders directly through our website

www.tempus-publishing.com